COIN AND PRECIOUS METAL VALUES 2010

★★★★★

TRENDS, DEALS, AND PREDICTIONS FOR THE SMART INVESTOR

COIN AND PRECIOUS METAL VALUES 2010

TRENDS, DEALS, AND PREDICTIONS FOR THE SMART INVESTOR

JIM KINGSLAND

House of Collectibles

NEW YORK   TORONTO   LONDON   SYDNEY   AUCKLAND

Important notice: All the information, including valuations, in this book has been compiled from reliable sources, and efforts have been made to eliminate errors and questionable data. Nevertheless, the possibility of error, in a work of such immense scope, always exists. The publisher will not be responsible for any losses that may occur in the purchase, sale, or other transaction of items because of information contained herein. Readers who feel they have discovered errors are invited to write and inform us, so they may be corrected in subsequent editions.

Copyright © 2010 by Jim Kingsland.

All rights reserved. Published in the United States by House of Collectibles, an imprint of The Random House Information Group, a division of Random House, Inc., New York, and in Canada by Random House of Canada Limited, Toronto.

House of Collectibles and colophon are registered trademarks of Random House, Inc.

RANDOM HOUSE is a registered trademark of Random House, Inc.

Please address inquiries about electronic licensing of any products for use on a network, in software, or on CD-ROM to the Subsidiary Rights Department, Random House Information Group, fax 212-572-6003.

This book is available for special discounts for bulk purchases for sales promotions or premiums. Special editions, including personalized covers, excerpts of existing books, and corporate imprints, can be created in large quantities for special needs. For more information, write to Random House, Inc., Special Markets/Premium Sales, 1745 Broadway, MD 6-2, New York, NY 10019 or e-mail specialmarkets@randomhouse.com

Visit the Random House Web site: www.randomhouse.com

Library of Congress Cataloging-in-Publication Data
Kingsland, Jim.
  Coin and precious metal values, 2010 : trends, deals, and predictions for the smart investor / Jim Kingsland.—1st ed.
     p.   cm.
  Includes bibliographical references and index.
  ISBN 978-0-375-72330-8 (alk. paper)
  1. Coins—Collectors and collecting—Handbooks, manuals, etc. 2. Precious metals—Handbooks, manuals, etc. 3. Coins—Prices—Handbooks, manuals, etc. I. Title.
  CJ81.K54 2009
  332.63—dc22   2009036263

ISBN: 978-0-375-72330-8

Printed in the United States

10 9 8 7 6 5 4 3 2 1

First Edition

CONTENTS

Foreword by Scott A. Travers — vii

Preface — xi

Introduction — xiii

   1. The Growing Lure of Coins and Precious Metals — 1

   2. Running With the Bulls — 27

   3. Making the Grade: Trends in Coin Grading — 41

   4. The Kingsland Collectibles Indices — 65

   5. Value Trends in Copper — 69

   6. Value Trends in Base Metal Alloy Coins — 79

   7. Value Trends in Silver — 89

   8. Value Trends in Gold — 107

   9. Value Trends in Platinum — 133

Appendix A: Coin Specifications — 141

Appendix B: Notable Coin-related Legislation — 159

Appendix C: Glossary — 179

Index — 197

Acknowledgments — 203

FOREWORD

by Scott A. Travers

We may not be in a depression these days in a strict economic sense, but we're certainly mighty depressed—and that dismal feeling stems from a four-letter word: debt.

DEBT could be an acronym for the problems that prompted Jim Kingsland to write this book, standing for Dilution of Equity, Bankruptcies, and Trust—or really, a lack of trust. These are the reasons people are buying gold and Treasury notes. What really got us into this mess, besides pure debt, were various offshoots of debt: derivatives, credit default swaps, and subprime mortgages. All of these are creative forms of debt.

Back in 1984, I wrote a book called *The Coin Collector's Survival Manual* in response to analogous problems in the rare coin industry. What we saw in the coin field then was what we are seeing now—and have been seeing for years—in the financial services industry. For many years, we had been seeing a lack of transparency: Collectors and investors were being told to buy coins as a long-term investment, and then, when they tried to sell those coins years later, they found that the coins were worth much less than they expected. The sellers had misrepresented the coins by overgrading and overpricing them; they had taken advantage of the often-uninformed buyers.

In *The Coin Collector's Survival Manual*, I told consumers things that dealers didn't want them to know. My book is widely credited with changing the landscape for collectors and investors and making coin consumers informed and knowledgeable. What *The Coin Collector's Survival Manual* did for the coin industry in creating transparency back in 1984, and blowing the lid off the buy-and-hold philosophy that merchants were touting to unknowledgeable investors, Jim Kingsland is doing now for investors in stocks and other traditional assets.

This is significant because Jim has had a long affiliation with global media outlets. He's viewed as an insider in the financial services "establishment," just as I was viewed as a coin market insider in 1984, when I exposed abuses in the coin industry. I applaud Jim for having the courage and integrity to come forward and educate investors. Like the old-time coin market, Wall Street is known for its buy-and-hold mentality—its goal is to keep you fully invested and tied to "the house." Jim's book reveals the flaws in this approach and shows how unconventional assets such as gold—widely disparaged by the Wall Street establishment—can be a much better bet in troubled times such as these.

Never before has a mainstream financial broadcast journalist with such a broad range of experience created such transparency for investors in every asset class, including coins and precious metals. Jim Kingsland was a direct hire of Mike Bloomberg and was Bloomberg Business Radio's morning drive anchor for a decade. He later served as Bloomberg's news director, then moved on to CNBC, where he applied his skills as a reporter. At News Corporation, he serves as assignment editor for the FOX Business Network and guest markets commentator for FOX Radio affiliates.

In August 2007, Jim predicted in his blog at JimKingsland.com that the Dow Jones Industrial Average would sink to 7,200 within the next couple of years. In that same blog, he said that gold would soar above one thousand dollars an ounce within the next year or two. Both of those forecasts—which skeptics considered dubious at the time—have come to pass. Jim went against the grain; at a time when many "experts," including others in the global financial media, were saying that stocks would surge in value, he correctly foresaw just the opposite. Unlike so many others, he recognized the bubble in stocks. And while others in the media were saying that gold would go lower and wasn't the place to be, Jim staked his reputation on a bold prediction that gold would rise above one thousand dollars.

The buy-and-hold mentality just won't work—and can't work—at a time of so much volatility. There's a different mood on Wall Street and a different approach is required. Some of the most perennially popular buy-and-hold stocks have abysmal track records lately. GM, Citigroup, Bank of America, General

Electric—all have been trading for just a small fraction of what they used to be. Lehman Brothers doesn't even exist anymore, and AIG has been effectively nationalized. Jim Kingsland foresaw such setbacks and expressed his concerns publicly and forthrightly in his online blog for all to see. And now he's pointing out ways that smart buyers can profit down the line from the extraordinary investment opportunities created by the market's current chaos.

Nowhere is Jim's advice more pertinent—and potentially more valuable—than in the case of gold. Focusing on the yellow metal's longtime role as a store of wealth and hedge against economic disaster, Jim shows why he believes that over the next several years, consumers will need to be prepared in ways they've never been before—including the possession of gold in physical form. This, he says, could be their number-one lifeline in case there is a breakdown of law and order, or the economic crisis deepens to the point where it threatens the nation's very future, unthinkable though that may seem even now.

As Jim points out, the value of all the mined gold in the world totals only about $5 trillion. That sum seems startlingly small when weighed against projections that it could cost somewhere between $3 trillion and $12 trillion to rescue the nation's banks. Above-ground stocks of gold total 162,000 metric tons, or 5.2 billion ounces, of which the United States holds about 261 million ounces and central banks of the world hold about 900 million ounces. Newly mined gold increases the overall supply by just 1.5 percent a year, but currency expands globally by 10 percent a year. Logically, then, gold should continue to rise in value, especially at a time when well-justified economic fears are fueling exceptional demand.

Some investors worry that the federal government may confiscate gold, as it did in the early 1930s. I have always regarded such fear as irrational. As I see it, the government is more likely to impose cumbersome reporting requirements in an effort to discourage investment in physical gold. In any event, collectible gold coins are unlikely to be subject to seizure; indeed, they were exempt even in the '30s, though much of the public wasn't aware of this and turned them in anyway.

Just how good an investment is gold today? One way to measure this is to see how gold stacks up against the Dow Jones average. In September 1929, when the Dow hit a high of 380, gold was $20.67 an ounce—a ratio of roughly 18:1. In July 1932, when the stock market hit rock bottom, with the Dow at 41.63 and gold fixed at $20.67, the ratio was 2:1. In January 1980, gold peaked at $887.50 an ounce on the international market and the Dow Jones was 867, so the ratio was 1:1. In July 1999, with the Dow at 11,210 and gold at $253 an ounce, the ratio was 44:1. As I write this, in February 2009, the Dow is at 7,355 and gold at $980 an ounce, for a ratio of 7.5:1.

The point of this exercise is that historically, when the stock market scales important highs, gold is at a low point—and when the Dow hits important lows, gold is at a high point. Because of the new lows in the stock market, we are seeing increasingly higher highs for gold. To get to a ratio of 2:1, stocks would have to go a lot lower and gold a lot higher.

Jim Kingsland points this out with courage, insight, and wisdom, but what makes his work so compelling—and provides a golden lining for the many dark storm clouds on the horizon—is that he presents all this in a way that will allow you to realize a profit. He conveys it constructively, not destructively, and shows you how to jump on the gold bandwagon, recognize which stocks are undervalued, and compare gold and coins to other asset classes—all the while explaining the perils and the pitfalls of investing in these various assets.

No other expert from a global media outlet has been willing to create the kind of transparency Jim Kingsland provides regarding stocks, bonds, and commodities. Jim has shown us clearly that what we are seeing with gold and other precious metals is not just a bubble, but a generational trend—and what we are seeing in the stock market is truly frightening.

Scott A. Travers
March 1, 2009
New York, NY

PREFACE

Since as far back as I can remember, I've had a love for coin collecting, which has evolved through the years to involve hedging risk in the financial markets. As a business journalist who has worked in senior editorial roles at the FOX Business Network and Bloomberg and CNBC, I've also had a fascination with numbers and data. Closer examination of the numbers helps to bring greater transparency to reporting. Combining my passion for coins with my penchant for numbers and experience as a financial journalist results in this book.

To keep abreast of the changing factors that impact coin and metals prices, this book will be updated yearly. Your criticisms, praises, feedback, and suggestions, sent directly to me at jim@jimkingsland.com, will be taken into account as I begin to develop *Coin and Precious Metal Values 2011: Trends, Deals, and Predictions for the Smart Investor*.

What I present to you here is general information based on my opinions and cannot take the place of personalized investment advice from a registered investment advisor. The information and analysis are derived from sources and methods believed to be reliable at the time of writing, but I strongly encourage you to consult with your own personal financial advisor before making investment decisions.

Here's to greater transparency and a better understanding of what makes the coin and metals markets tick!

Jim Kingsland
June 15, 2009
New York, NY

INTRODUCTION

What could be unique about yet another among the hundreds of coin books that have been written over the last decade—another voice amidst the many eloquent spokespeople who represent or write about the coin industry? For starters, this isn't just a book about coins. It's a book about investments—in both coins and precious metals. It goes beyond examining trends in the buying and selling of coins, to take on the complicated factors that affect the rise and fall of the metals from which the coins are made—factors ranging from unbridled U.S. federal spending and fluctuations in the currency and bond and stock markets to the economic health of the United States and Europe, technological and industrial demand for metals, and the logistics of extracting these metals from the earth.

Why focus on coins rather than devise cheeky ideas for finding the next mega-investing trend in a burned and land-mined stock-market environment? It's simple: Investing in coins and gold and silver bullion has worked well for those who have done their homework and shunned an orchestrated effort by Wall Street's biggest and most infamous individuals and institutions to capture investment dollars with spurious claims of outperformance, always disclaimed with "past performance is no guarantee of future results."

Those results are now plain to see: The well-dressed and grossly compensated operators of what turned out to be nothing more than lower-Manhattan-skyscraper-based bucket shops and boiler rooms saw their firms come tumbling down. They cling to their existence on financial life support thanks to present and future American taxpayers, millions of whom (even many yet to be born) will end up paying dearly for the crash of 2008. The upswing in popularity of investments in coins and precious metals and the effects of the current economic downturn on investor confidence is the subject of chapter 1, "The Growing Lure of Coins and Precious Metals."

This is also a book about trends. Has the trend been your friend, as the old Wall Street saying goes, or were you caught completely off guard when the stock market crashed? It bears mentioning that the word "trend" is often misused by the day-trading crowd to mean something more than an hour but less than a trading day. For the purposes of this book and to be fair, we'll look at trends from a perspective of at least ten years—a common benchmark employed by what used to be touted as the all-knowing and all-safe mutual-fund industry. The ten-year time frame has often been used to "smooth" out performance measurements.

Today many investors are licking serious wounds inflicted by that industry and the mantra of buy, buy, buy, and then hold, hold, hold, with no fire escape provided. When ensuring the financial well-being of their clients meant yelling "sell!" in their own crowded investor "theaters," mutual-fund companies failed to do so, and now millions are wondering how they'll retire. As chapter 2, "Running With the Bulls," shows, mutual funds have failed while metals have rallied.

In the pages ahead, you'll find the largely untold story of why coins have been a good friend to investors over the last ten years, and especially in the last three years of volatile stock and bond prices. (A look at the trends in coin grading and a "101" for new coin investors is the basis for chapter 3.) I'll also impart a muffled truth about precious metals: Despite what you may have seen on TV or read in the newspapers, gold, silver, and their base-metal cousins are not investment also-rans. The world isn't all about stocks, and as stock investors reckon with harsh losses, they should assess the many examples of historically strong investment performance for precious metals.

For good measure this book also examines how metals impact coin prices and compares both coins and metals to stocks, bonds, and currencies, as well as to real estate and art. Chapters 5 through 9 detail market trends, performance, and outlooks for copper, silver, gold, and platinum, as well as base-metal alloy coins.

Doing just a bit of excavation into the financial landscape digs up data revealing just how well metals have performed. Sure, they've had their ups and downs like any other investment, but overall, the returns are positive in gold and silver while stocks have suffered greatly this past year and have underperformed even over the longer haul (the past ten years) relative to pundit- and TV-analyst predictions.

This may seem like an all-out assault on the stock market. Not exactly. I realize that stocks will always be around, but I question whether too many eggs have been placed in the stocks basket. Admittedly, this is a polarizing question for those deeply vested in stocks and who want it all. In this book, I let the pieces, or in this case the numbers, fall where they may. These have been trying times for investors, and now more than ever we need clarity on what to do in the aftermath of 2008's stock-market meltdown. Stocks are not the only hope for the future—other investments can be a piece of a puzzle to repair a broken portfolio.

A good and ominous reason why metals have taken off in recent years is the broad-based economic factors at play—another focus of this book. I'll examine how the dollar's future on the world stage and whether the United States will bankrupt itself through unchecked spending to arrest the financial crisis—issues that will impact our financial lives for decades to come—play into the outlook for coins and metals. You will also discover how the current bevy of financial bailouts and aid packages are affecting the trend in gold and other metals prices.

Throughout the book, names that make the news—experts in the field of coins and precious metals—weigh in on market dynamics. Among them is John Albanese, the founder of the coin verification service CAC and a giant in the coin world—a renowned expert who was the cofounder of grading giant PCGS. We also hear from Mark Salzberg, the chairman of coin-grading juggernaut Numismatic Guaranty Corporation, who shares his insights on the process of grading coins, coin market conditions, and some strong opinions on smaller, or what he calls "third-world," coin-grading services. Author, coin expert, attorney, and for decades a numismatic journalist, David L. Ganz offers his analysis about a bad memory for gold investors: confiscation. Can it happen again? David fills us in. Last but certainly not least, coin expert, dealer, and renowned coin author Scott A. Travers provides thoughts on where some of the hot opportunities exist for coin investors and hobbyists. Scott was also gracious enough to pen the foreword to this book.

In poring over the data, I've come to realize that gauges of information on collectibles and assets are not readily available. Google searches yield bits and pieces of data; in this day and age there ought to be an easier way to get the pulse on nontraditional markets. To that end, in chapter 4, I introduce the Kingsland Asset Indices, the only indices of their kind, which track the prices of collectibles on the world market. The Kingsland Indices will appear at jimkingsland.com.

Looming over everything within these pages is the economic crisis gripping the nation and the world. Where did it come from and when will it go away? You'll get a viewpoint that you probably haven't read in the morning paper. Are the Washington politicians, the regulators, and the New York titans of business capable of tackling the situation and winning, or are the problems much bigger than advertised?

Be prepared for some sobering realities. If you've had a steady diet of stock-promoting television shows, you might not like what's ahead in these pages. It's a big financial world out there—a world with many more options than investing in stocks. Perhaps for just a short time, you'll tune out the talking heads, who still proclaim stock-buying opportunities any chance they get. This book is meant to serve as a guide to other investing ideas by portraying the real investment success stories of the last decade along with the failures.

1

THE GROWING LURE OF COINS AND PRECIOUS METALS

Real estate dead zones pockmarked the nation as the Great Recession entered 2009, and one of the biggest was in the state of Nevada. Unbridled speculation had led to the creation of false wealth in the Silver State, and this illusory "boom" turned into a bust that was just about as bad as a bust can get. The collapse of real estate left the state fighting budget deficits in the hundreds of millions of dollars and saddled with a seemingly endless landscape of foreclosed homes.

But amid this misery there was one little town in Nevada with a happy story line. The town is Battle Mountain, population four thousand, in Lander County, about two hundred miles east of Reno, off an isolated exit on the transcontinental Interstate 80. Battle Mountain is enjoying boom times thanks to gold mining. It is home to the old Battle Mountain Gold company, which was swallowed up some years ago in a merger with Newmont Mining, currently the world's largest gold producer.

Battle Mountain and its newfound prosperity caught the eye of the *New York Times*, which profiled the town in an upbeat article in January 2009. While there's little to see and do there, the town boasted an unemployment rate of about half the statewide average and almost no home foreclosures—even as Nevada held the dubious distinction of being the state with the most home foreclosures for twenty-three consecutive months at the time the article was published. Both Newmont Mining and a competitor, Barrick, have complained that there aren't enough workers available in the area to keep up with twenty-four/seven mining operations that yield more than a million ounces of gold per year.

The boom is a nice change of pace for a county that has suffered through bust times as well. A decade earlier, when gold was flirting with $230 an ounce, the mines were laying off workers and small businesses in town were shutting down. Now, businesses are coming back. Said one local quoted in the *Times* report, "In tough times, people need a backup for their money, and that backup is gold."

As the economic crisis persists and the dollar sags, investors are flocking to coins and precious metals. Just how bad is the fiscal state of affairs, and what's ahead? Those are key questions in determining longer-term trends, and answering them will help to tune out much of the noise that still emanates from the Wall Street television pundits who declare, every chance they get, that "it's now a buying opportunity for stocks," or that "we've hit bottom."

AS THE MARKET FLOUNDERS, INVESTORS FLOCK TO TANGIBLE ASSETS

For all too many American workers, 2008 and 2009 saw 401(k) plans reduced to 201(k)—or even 101(k)—plans. Complacent employees who thought their retirement nest eggs would perpetually grow, suddenly faced losses of 40 percent or more—with the huge financial cuts coming not in the space of years, but in the course of just a few months. Adding insult to injury, while 401(k) values were collapsing, housing prices plummeted, and then the pool of available jobs also crashed.

■ NATIONAL AVERAGE HOME PRICE

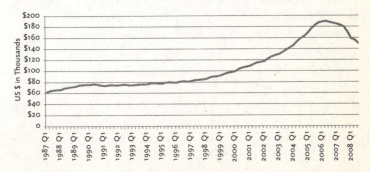

National Average Home Price. Home equity has been lost since the boom went bust, and declines in home prices show no signs of abating. The data from S&P's Case-Schiller index show home prices are in a state of freefall as a seemingly unending supply of homes floods the market. *Data source: Standard and Poor's*

■ DOW JONES INDUSTRIALS—A FAST TRIP DOWN

A Stock Market Crash in a Matter of Months. The downturn in the market that caught many off-guard has left benchmark stock indexes hanging by a thread to lows not seen since the dot-com bust. *Data source: Dow Jones*

■ NONFARM JOBS CREATION

Nonfarm Jobs Creation: From Financial Assets to Labor Market Cuts. Americans are coping not only with huge investment losses, but also with major setbacks in the labor market, where 2.6 million jobs were lost in 2008. *Data source: U.S. Department of Labor*

To put it another way, in just the first quarter of 2009, the Federal Reserve reported a drop in household wealth of over $1 trillion, marking a seventh straight quarterly decline. Household wealth peaked in the spring of 2007 at over $60 trillion and now stands at just over $50 trillion.

President Obama has acknowledged the unstable state of the country's fiscal affairs by stating that "we're out of money." Fed chairman Ben Bernanke has also warned of a bleak economic outlook and has told Washington that "hard choices" need to be made to cut federal deficits or the economy will become increasingly unstable. Notable investment experts have also fanned the flames. When the masses hear a commodities and currency guru such as Jimmy Rogers say on the Bloomberg News Service that "the U.K. is finished" and "the dollar is doomed," investors take notice and want in on paper securities alternatives like gold.

Overwhelmingly, coin collectors and metals investors have responded to the current economic rough patch by buying up whatever output mines can produce. A herd mentality clearly has developed. The World Gold Council shows a nearly 250 percent year-over-year jump in investment demand for gold during just the first quarter of 2009. Investors up to the billionaire level are leading the charge into coins and metals. They understand the precarious position of the world financial system and appreciate the inherent weaknesses still menacing Main Street American investors even after surviving the stock market collapse of 2008 and early 2009. With confidence in financial systems and in the regulators who oversee them at all-time lows, metals in both coin and bullion form have come to the fore.

COIN COLLECTING MORE POPULAR THAN EVER

Coin collecting is booming. Brisk demand for coins has been reported at both local and large coin shows. Bidding has been strong even at the top end—six figures and beyond for truly rare coins. Demand has been so high for bullion coins that the U.S. Mint has had to cancel several offerings of gold, silver, and platinum bullion products. By some estimates, acquiring collectible coins—as both a hobby and an investment—has attracted 150 million people in the United States alone over the past decade. New enthusiasts sprout up every day, drawn by the love of coins themselves, the prospect of fending off economic setbacks, or both. With the stock-centric world a thing of the past, growing numbers of investors are turning their attention to gold and silver coins and bullion as hedges against potential inflation, further economic collapse, and whatever other financial bogeymen are lurking in the closet.

Collectors come from all walks of life, ranging from a child who's filling a 50 State Quarters album with help from Mom and Dad, to someone who finds an old coin in his pocket change, to a hobbyist who has spent a lifetime building a coin set. More and more people have been buying late nineteenth- and early twentieth-century U.S. gold coins to diversify their assets and/or as a form of insurance against economic calamity.

PRECIOUS METALS INVESTING ON THE RISE

Investor demand for gold and silver is also at record levels. The U.K.'s *Telegraph* pulled no punches in early 2009 with this blaring headline: "Merrill Lynch Says Rich Turning to Gold Bars For Safety." According to its report, some of the financial services company's wealthiest clients had started moving away from paper derivatives and toward physical gold. The report quoted Merrill Lynch's chief investment officer, Gary Dugan, as saying, "It is amazing how many clients want physical gold, not ETFs [exchange trade funds listed in London, New York, and on other bourses]. They are so worried they want a portable asset in their house. I never thought I would be getting calls from clients saying they want a box of Krugerrands."

Coin authority Scott Travers (author of this book's foreword) says demand encompasses not only bullion but also U.S. $20 gold Eagles—gold coins struck in the late 1800s and early 1900s, with nearly an ounce of gold and a face value of $20.

"I've never seen anything like this," said Travers, author of *The Coin Collector's Survival Manual*, noting that the fervor for gold now has far surpassed that of 1979 and 1980, when people rushed to tangible assets in light of gas shortages, inflation, and skyrocketing interest rates.

"Physical gold does well in times of economic distress, calamity, and blood in the streets," Travers added. "Gold is really a quasi-currency as people worry about a possible collapse of the banking system."

UNDERSTANDING MONEY

To better comprehend what's driving the huge demand for gold and silver, it's important to understand how money is valued, or more precisely what is likely to devalue the dollars that sit in depositories, from the wallet to the bank vaults of the world. Understanding money requires an understanding of who controls the money supply, which in the United States falls to the Federal Reserve.

WHAT IS THE FEDERAL RESERVE?

A Google search for "Jekyll Island" returns a number of results concerning a beautiful island resort just off the Georgia coast. But adding the word "Fed" to the search opens a portal to articles on a series of then-secret meetings in 1910 that led to creation of the Federal Reserve System, the central bank of the United States.

The Fed was founded in 1913 by Congress in order to, in its own words, "provide the nation with a safer, more flexible, and more stable monetary and financial system."

Today, the Federal Reserve's duties fall into four general areas:

- Conducting the nation's monetary policy by influencing the monetary and credit conditions in the economy in pursuit of maximum employment, stable prices, and moderate long-term interest rates

- Supervising and regulating banking institutions to ensure the safety and soundness of the nation's banking and financial system and to protect the credit rights of consumers

- Maintaining the stability of the financial system and containing systemic risk that may arise in financial markets

- Providing financial services to depository institutions, the U.S. government, and foreign official institutions, including playing a major role in operating the nation's payments system.

Most developed countries have a central bank whose functions are broadly similar to those of the Federal Reserve. The Fed is a relatively young central bank. The world's oldest central bank, Sweden's Riksbank, has existed since 1668, and the Bank of England was founded in 1694. Napoleon I established the Banque de France in 1800, and the Bank of Canada began operations in 1935. The German Bundesbank was reestablished after World War II and is loosely modeled on the Federal Reserve. More recently, some functions of the Banque de France and the Bundesbank have been assumed by the European Central Bank, formed in 1998.

G. Edward Griffin, author of *The Creature from Jekyll Island*, a comprehensive history of the Federal Reserve's founding, says there's a lot more to the story of the Federal Reserve. He maintains the Fed was founded by a group of bankers who wanted to centralize control of the banking system. Jekyll Island, according to Griffin, was the secret meeting location for the bankers and senators who gathered in 1910 to formulate plans for the central bank.

Griffin says the upshot of the creation of the Fed has been inflation, or diminished buying power for all due to the Fed's ability to create money at its own will. Griffin is on to something, considering that the dollar's buying power today is a fraction of what it was when the Fed was created. Today, $150,000 will barely pay for the land to build a McMansion in some areas, while at the turn of the twentieth century $150,000 would get you a real and majestic mansion. Prior to the Fed's creation, aside from fluctuations during the Civil War years and during the 1837 to 1844 depression years, the dollar's buying power remained relatively unchanged from the creation of the Republic.

This leads to an important question: What—beyond the dictionary definition of "a medium of exchange for goods and services"—is money? For the purposes of this book, we consider two types of money: sound money, which is backed by a commodity like gold or silver; and fiat money, backed by nothing but what society feels its value ought to be.

We live in an era of fiat money, but we weren't the first.

Anything but a Roman Delight

Ancient Rome stands out as an enduring example, albeit an extreme one, of how a country's money can be devalued and then ultimately becomes worthless. U.S. Comptroller David Walker (now retired) regularly compared the United States to ancient Rome before its fall, saying the United States has a "broken business model." Well before bailouts and special lending programs to keep banking institutions alive and cash flowing through them, the Term Asset-Backed Securities Loan Facility (TALF), the Troubled Asset Relief Program (TARP), and unrestrained Federal Reserve money printing, Walker worried about future Medicare and Social Security promises. "We face a massive demographic tsunami that will never recede," he said at the time.

The debasement (drop in value) of Roman money nearly 2,000 years ago and the problems arising today from serious financial dislocations and lack of fiscal restraint do have similar characteristics.

By 300 A.D., Roman society was torn asunder by a variety of social and fiscal ills. A steady stream of emperors found that maintaining an empire was a very expensive proposition. External security demands and a blooming internal welfare state were straining the empire's coffers. It was deficit spending, Roman-style. Emperors ended up doing what many rulers have done in now-defunct empires, kingdoms, and nations: They created more "money" and in doing so devalued their currencies. In the short term, more money would be available, but the money was worth less and eventually would become totally worthless.

Silver, in the form of the denarius (a silver coin), was the workhorse of the Roman financial system. As more denarii were created to keep the empire afloat, the value of the money decreased and merchants were left with no choice but to raise prices. With inflation, the real trap is that wages don't go up in proportion to rising prices, making the cost of living a greater burden. In order to prevent a silver shortage with the flurry of new money, the Romans had to reduce the size and silver content of the denarius, creating the first fiat currency.

INFLATION—THE QUICK WAY TO MAKE LIFE ROTTEN

Gasoline's surge to four dollars a gallon in 2008 was a stark example of inflation's terrible impact. As the value of U.S. dollars fell at the start of the twenty-first century, commodities priced in dollars became more expensive due to the dollar's diminished buying power. While the price of gasoline doubled for a time, wages certainly didn't keep up, so dollars going into gas tanks left less to spend on other commodities. At the same time, industries reliant upon energy (pretty much every industry) were stung by higher energy costs, which were passed along through the entire supply-and-consumption chain.

A word that's being bandied about these days has even more alarming connotations: hyperinflation. With hyperinflation, money becomes so valueless that it's pretty much impossible to buy anything. Picture the wheelbarrow full of cash that was needed to buy a loaf of bread in Germany during the early 1920s. Lately, hyperinflation has been running rampant in the African nation of Zimbabwe, where in 2008 the broad money supply rose by an inconceivable 231 million percent in the space of months—to the point where a loaf of bread cost 300 billion Zimbabwean dollars. Likewise, Iceland's currency, after its collapse in late 2008, was worth only 40 percent of its pre-collapse value.

By 300 A.D., the government of Rome was so overstretched that its "silver" coinage contained just a tiny fraction of precious metal. Often a silver coin was no more than a bronze coin dipped in silver—and even that pretense eventually was abandoned. Roman money had been devalued to the point of worthlessness.

ROMAN DENARIUS SILVER CONTENT

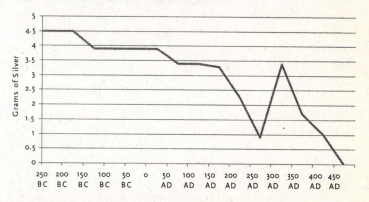

The Death of the Denarius. The workhorse of the Roman monetary system for five hundred years started out strong, with high silver content. By the third century A.D. it was replaced by a copper coin called the aurelien, which had just a silver wash. In currency terms, it was a slow and painful death.

During Rome's tumultuous inflationary period when silver coinage faltered, its gold aureus, composed of genuine gold, remained available in limited quantities. This enabled Rome to pay certain segments of the population, such as the army and key trading partners, with coins of true value. The silver denarius rapidly lost value, starting in the fourth century. Early on, a single gold aureus was equivalent in value to about eight hundred silver coins. Within fifty years, an aureus was exchangeable for a whopping 4.6 million Roman silver pieces.

The devalued pieces came to be known as "waning silver" coins. And despite being minted more than fifteen hundred years ago, this type of Roman coinage remains almost worthless to this day. Dealers offer the coins for as little as nine dollars each.

Ultimately, large pockets of Roman society turned to the inefficient and oppressive system of bartering for goods and services instead of using the official but worthless coinage. While many reasons are given for the slow and miserable death of the Roman Empire, the economic collapse caused by valueless money stands out as a key factor in the empire's demise.

Rome's experience serves as an important object lesson on the value of keeping precious-metal coinage pure, and the perils of debasing it.

The True Story of Paper Money

Today we are all fiat. The more than 300 million U.S. citizens collectively agree without even really thinking about it that one dollar, with the backing of nothing, buys one dollar's worth of goods or services. No country currently backs its currency with any sort of gold or silver standard. President Richard M. Nixon unilaterally closed what was known as the gold window in 1971, ending the fractional gold standard that the United States used after World War II. U.S. gold reserves were being depleted rapidly because foreign trading partners preferred and demanded gold over an increasing supply of U.S. paper money as a means of settling our balance of payments. Nixon saw little choice but to end the gold standard, which he did without congressional approval.

Fat Fiat Times

On the morning after the gold window was closed in 1971, something dramatic and yet unremarkable happened, as it had for billions of years: The sun rose from out of the eastern sky. America was off the gold standard, and still, society as we knew it continued. The size of the American economy would go on to double, triple, quadruple, and ultimately grow by more than eleven-fold over the next four decades to present day.

Many indicators point to a great degree of prosperity, or at least abundant middle-class comfort and growth during this period of fiat money. But while the financial world didn't come to an end in the short term, the temptation for and ability of the government to borrow and spend at will under a fiat currency system eventually caught up with the United States. While Gross Domestic Product totaled more than $13 trillion in 2008, up from just over $1 trillion at the start of the 1970s, the national debt expanded to more than $12 trillion. Chickens were coming home to roost, and that increased the appeal of gold and silver ownership.

Fiat with a Long-Term Inflation Bite

Our fiat currency system has come with another big price tag: debased U.S. currency. The estimated $1-trillion-plus money supply that flies around our planet is still quite spendable and can be converted to a host of other currencies such as the yen, the euro, and scores of others. The dollar gets you much less today, though, than it did in 1970, the year before Nixon closed the window. According to the Cleveland Federal Reserve Bank's inflation calculator, $250 of anything in today's money, including groceries, would have cost only forty dollars in 1971 dollars.

Additionally, the inflation that has resulted since the closing of the gold window has stymied wages. Between 1972 and 2008, real earned income—a gauge of wages adjusted for inflation—has fallen 16 percent. This has led to a nasty long-term cycle of a falling savings rate and an increase of debt taken on by consumers to make up for the loss in real earned income.

Still, during the current financial crisis the dollar has held remarkably steady, and even as an ever-greater supply of dollars is printed, the dollar has held onto its post–World War II status as the reserve currency of the world. What is a reserve currency? Investopedia.com defines it as "a foreign currency held by central banks and other major financial institutions as a means to pay off international debt obligations, or to influence their domestic exchange rate." It adds: "Currently, the U.S. dollar is the primary reserve currency used by other countries. A very large percentage of commodities such as gold and oil are usually priced in U.S dollars."

The U.S. Dollar Index, shown below, is a trade-weighted index of six currencies that was created by the Federal Reserve in March 1973 using the fixed exchange rates set by the 1944 Bretton Woods agreement. The index is calculated today with a geometric formula using current exchange rates, comparing current data against the starting or "zero" point of March 1973 when the U.S. dollar was set at a value of one hundred.

■ **THE DOLLAR INDEX**

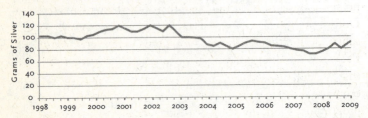

The Dollar Remains a Survivor. The Dollar Index is a gauge of the buck's strength against a basket of key currencies, including the yen and euro. The index shows the dollar's overall downward trend since 1998.

Currency weights, or the amount of foreign currencies used versus the dollar to calculate the index, in the Dollar Index are as follows: euro = 57.6 percent, Canadian dollar = 9.1 percent, Japanese yen = 13.6 percent, Swedish krona = 4.2 percent, British pound = 11.9 percent, Swiss franc = 3.6 percent. Had there been a greater weighting in yen as opposed to euros, the Dollar Index would be weaker than it is now since the yen has been stronger than the euro.

The dollar's designation as a reserve currency has given the United States virtual free rein over how many dollars it can print. In mid-2009, as the dollar continued to enjoy reserve currency status, its value had actually rebounded from the lows of 2008 as it retained remarkable safe-haven status. However, as the reality of a $2 trillion federal budget deficit for fiscal 2010 has taken hold, the dollar has fallen steadily in 2009, and the question that becomes louder each day is how long the dollar will remain stable and hold its reserve currency status. It's the ghosts of currencies past that cast doubt on whether the future of the dollar will be bright.

Paper Currencies Are Mortal

Many observers, including those actively buying gold, question just how long the U.S. can get away with unlimited printing of dollars. Will the dollar lose its reserve currency status? Many say no, simply because at the moment there is no better game around. Dollar pundits reason that the euro would not be a strong enough substitute and that it's too early for China to take up the currency slack. For now, the dollar reigns supreme. But this is not to say that the dollar won't lose still more spending power as the government and the Federal Reserve commit to further actions to prop up the economy. Regional currency alternatives could also be set up in different parts of the world. Members of certain industries, such as the oil industry, could choose on their own to decouple from the dollar and accept payments only in another currency such as the euro.

According to the Web site dollardaze.org, which tracks the life and death of currencies, "the median age for all existing currencies in circulation is only thirty-nine years." The Web site's study of 599 currencies that no longer circulate shows a median age of just fifteen years. Another study of 775 currencies shows that 20 percent of the now-dead currencies were destroyed by hyperinflation.

The dollar has had an amazing run that dates back to 1792—making it the third-oldest currency in the world, trailing only the British pound (circulated since 1694) and the Scottish pound (since 1727). But the dollar was a gold-standard currency through most of that time, until 1971. Frame the dollar in a different light—that of a fiat currency born in 1971—and it matches the median age of thirty-nine years for currencies now in existence.

Metals investors reason that a day of reckoning lies ahead for the dollar. And if not a day of reckoning and ruin, then enough devaluation to make coins and bullion beneficial in the unchartered territory where the dollar is likely to find itself as the financial crisis continues.

It's no wonder, then, that financial heavyweights are becoming vocal champions of coins and precious metals. Figures from the World Gold Council and U.S. Mint aren't a predictor of the dollar's longevity, but they show unprecedented investor demand for these assets.

HUGE DEFICITS FOR YEARS TO COME

The cost of addressing the present crisis, plus obligations made in the past, could trigger a breaking point for the U.S. dollar as trillion-dollar phraseology becomes routine when discussing fiscal matters and bailouts. Federal budget deficits using generally accepted accounting principles (GAAP; accounting rules used by corporations) are projected to exceed $5 trillion a year—as far as the mind's eye can see—when Social Security and Medicare liabilities are factored in. According to the Congressional Budget Office, the United States has a negative net worth approaching $60 trillion and long-term liabilities of nearly $70 trillion for programs it has promised to fund, including future Social Security and Medicare spending.

The United States has opted to pay its bills and carry out gargantuan bailouts through the printing of dollars, or paper backed by nothing, and the results have begun to show up in data such as the Fed's monetary base statistics—the volume of money in the economy.

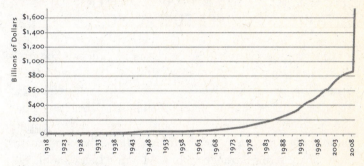

■ ADJUSTED MONETARY BASE (AMBNS)

Is America Spending Itself to Death? Figures provided by the Federal Reserve Bank of St. Louis are an ongoing chronicle of a deteriorating U.S. balance sheet. The bank releases a variety of measures of monetary health. In this chart going back to 1918, money growth moved at a fairly even keel for nearly 70 years, but took a more urgent upward turn as deficit spending increased. In the blink of an eye, the Fed flooded the monetary system in 2008 and grew the monetary base from roughly $800 billion to $1.7 trillion. *Data source: St. Louis Federal Reserve Bank*

Investor demand for gold and silver coins and precious metals themselves has been driven by the dual realities of weakening economies and the central banking remedy of liquefying, or flooding the global monetary system with cash.

Historically, governments have tried to walk a fine line between overly restricting a money supply, which can slow economic growth, and opening the money-creation spigot to the point where it creates an inflationary spiral that forces prices higher and reduces currency's spending power. The economic jigsaw puzzle confronting world monetary leaders today requires them not only to achieve economic balance and recovery, but also to shore up the foundation of the global currency system, which has been weakened by years of deficit spending that created mountainous debt. The growing number of people who are driving unprecedented demand for silver and gold are turning thumbs down on the multitrillion-dollar bailout schemes engineered by central banks around the globe—not the least of them, the U.S. Federal Reserve System.

THE U.S. REMAINS AN AAA COUNTRY, BUT QUESTIONS ARE SURFACING

This brings us to the ultimate question: Will this country's credit rating take a hit? As of this writing, the U.S. credit rating as rated by Standard & Poor's, Moody's, and Fitch remains at Aaa with a stable outlook. Aaa is the highest debt rating a nation can receive. It means the nation's sovereign debt is among the least risky to own. A stable outlook, after a thorough analysis, means a ratings agency such as Moody's Investors Service isn't about to downgrade Uncle Sam's triple-A status—which, in turn, means the U.S. Treasury should be able to sell notes, bills, and bonds at low interest rates. But as of this writing, the nation's balance sheet (also known as the "full faith and credit" of Uncle Sam) has been gaining greater attention. So what if Moody's and others say the United States is Aaa, given the near-scandalous assignment of Aaa ratings to billions of dollars of mortgage-backed securities that have since become virtually worthless?

Will there come a day when the United States finds itself in the difficult position of having to pay a higher cost of capital if it loses its coveted Aaa status, or if creditor nations that buy our Treasury securities launch a buyers' strike and demand a higher rate of return in response to a hobbled U.S. balance sheet?

Early in 2009, Moody's said the financial position of the United States will "worsen considerably over the coming two years" due to the recession and to the costs of fiscal stimulus and aid to financial institutions. Moody's went on to state that debt borrowed from creditors outside the federal government as of the end of 2008 "amounted to $5.8 trillion, equivalent to 40.8% of U.S. GDP." It described this as a moderate level, but cautioned that "total debt held by the public is projected to rise by more than half during the coming two years, reaching $9.0 trillion, or 62 percent of GDP, by the end of fiscal year 2010." To boil those numbers down, the United States faces a burdensome debt situation with no relief in sight.

To make the cheese more binding, Moody's cited a plethora of other data that should further drain investor confidence in the U.S. balance sheet and heighten the appeal of coins and precious metals. It took special note of "the ratio of this debt to the federal government's own revenue, which is a measure of the resources available at any moment to repay the debt."

"At the end of fiscal year 2008," Moody's stated, "the ratio was 230%, quite high for an Aaa-rated country. Moreover, this is also forecast to rise steeply in the next two years, reaching 378% by the end of fiscal year 2010. The burden of the debt, measured as the ratio of interest paid to the government's revenue, is another important indicator. In fiscal year 2009, this ratio is projected at about 9.5%, also a high level among Aaa countries."

Moody's also warned of other negative factors. "Treasury purchases of GSE [Fannie Mae and Freddie Mac] preferred stock and purchases under the Troubled Asset Relief Program (TARP) of commercial bank preferred stock and, possibly, mortgage-backed or other securities are set to have an adverse impact on the U.S. government financial position," the rating service said. "Moody's notes that the gross debt will also be increased by the fiscal stimulus package proposed by the incoming administration, now estimated at $825 billion over the next two years. However, it should also be noted that the possible future disposal of assets acquired by the government through its measures to aid the financial sector may affect the rating agency's opinion of whether the upward trend in debt ratios is reversible. Moody's further cautions that, whether in 2010 or after, interest rates are almost certain to rise from their current low levels and the affordability of the federal government debt will deteriorate."

To some, it was disturbing that Moody's saw the need to reiterate that it foresaw a stable outlook for the U.S. balance sheet. Quipped one Wall Street trader on financial television, "It's spooky that they even have to bring up this issue."

There will likely come a day when the U.S. credit rating is reviewed, especially if deficit spending is not curbed. Already, in the U.K. the British triple-A could be put under review by Standard & Poor's—how many years or months the United States is behind the U.K. remains to be seen.

BERNANKE'S PLAYBOOK

Americans have witnessed epic economic crises since mid-2008: a monumental correction in commodities prices, the collapse of major assets held by banks, the rapid decline of the banks themselves, the steep slide in real estate values and the values of many other assets. It can easily be argued that the world economy is in the throes of disinflation (previous inflationary pressure being wiped out of the economy) if not all-out deflation (where asset values fall and production capacity is idled). Federal Reserve Board Chairman Ben Bernanke's goal is to ensure market stability to the best of the Fed's ability and—extremely important for investors in coins and metals—to ensure that the U.S. economy doesn't plunge into a deflationary spiral.

When he was a Fed governor in 2002, Bernanke outlined a series of measures that would need to be taken to stop deflation dead in its tracks. His ideas were presented in a speech titled "Deflation: Making Sure 'It' Doesn't Happen Here" (contained in the archives of the Federal Reserve Board, available online at *www.federalreserve.gov/boardDocs/speeches/2002/20021121*), now widely referred to as "Bernanke's playbook," in which he famously cited the printing press, to create dollars, as but one of his tools in his arsenal to combat deflation. For those who feel the Fed is now a toothless tiger, the printing press issue alone raises an important question: How big is your printing press compared with that of the Fed chairman?

Bernanke's playbook discusses how the Fed might lower long-term rates. Bernanke is clearly convinced that the central bank can defeat inflation and he will do everything possible to defeat deflation—a positive trend for bullion and coins.

> The conclusion that deflation is always reversible under a fiat money system follows from basic economic reasoning. A little parable may prove useful: Today an ounce of gold sells for $300, more or less. Now suppose that a modern alchemist solves his subject's oldest problem by finding a way to produce unlimited amounts of new gold at essentially no cost. Moreover, his invention is widely publicized and scientifically verified, and he announces his intention to begin massive production of gold within days. What would happen to the price of gold? Presumably, the potentially unlimited supply of cheap gold would cause the market price of gold to plummet. Indeed, if the market for gold is to any degree efficient, the price of gold would collapse immediately after the announcement of the invention, before the alchemist had produced and marketed a single ounce of yellow metal.
>
> What has this got to do with monetary policy? Like gold, U.S. dollars have value only to the extent that they are strictly limited in supply. But the U.S. government has a technology, called a printing press (or, today, its electronic equivalent), that allows it to produce as many U.S. dollars as it wishes at essentially no cost. By increasing the number of U.S. dollars in circulation, or even by credibly threatening to do so, the U.S. government can also reduce the value of a dollar in terms of goods and services, which is equivalent to raising the prices in dollars of those goods and services. We conclude that, under a paper-money system, a determined government can always generate higher spending and hence positive inflation.

From these remarks, we can only surmise that Bernanke may be distressed that deflationary forces have already taken hold. But again, he expresses confidence that deflation is reversible:

> Of course, the U.S. government is not going to print money and distribute it willy-nilly (although, as we will see later, there are practical policies that approximate this behavior). Normally, money is injected into the economy through asset purchases by the Federal Reserve. To stimulate aggregate spending when short-term interest rates have reached zero, the Fed must expand the scale of its asset purchases or, possibly, expand the menu of assets that it buys. Alternatively, the Fed could find other ways of injecting money into the system—for example, by making low-interest-rate loans to banks or cooperating with the fiscal authorities. Each method of adding money to the economy has advantages and drawbacks, both technical and economic. One important concern in practice is that calibrating the economic effects of nonstandard means of injecting money may be difficult, given our relative lack of experience with such policies. Thus, as I have stressed already, prevention of deflation remains preferable to having to cure it. If we do fall into deflation, however, we can take comfort that the logic of the printing press example must assert itself, and sufficient injections of money will ultimately always reverse a deflation.

Bear in mind, this speech was delivered in 2002, yet Bernanke was outlining precisely the situation we see occurring now. He said the Fed could go so far as to buy longer-term Treasuries:

> So what then might the Fed do if its target interest rate, the overnight federal funds rate, fell to zero? One relatively straightforward extension of current procedures would be to try to stimulate spending by lowering rates further out along the Treasury term structure—that is, rates on government bonds of longer maturities. There are at least two ways of bringing down longer-term rates, which are complementary and could be employed separately

or in combination. One approach, similar to an action taken in the past couple of years by the Bank of Japan, would be for the Fed to commit to holding the overnight rate at zero for some specified period. Because long-term interest rates represent averages of current and expected future short-term rates, plus a term premium, a commitment to keep short-term rates at zero for some time—if it were credible—would induce a decline in longer-term rates. A more direct method, which I personally prefer, would be for the Fed to begin announcing explicit ceilings for yields on longer-maturity Treasury debt (say, bonds maturing within the next two years). The Fed could enforce these interest-rate ceilings by committing to make unlimited purchases of securities up to two years from maturity at prices consistent with the targeted yields. If this program were successful, not only would yields on medium-term Treasury securities fall, but (because of links operating through expectations of future interest rates) yields on longer-term public and private debt (such as mortgages) would likely fall as well.

Lower rates over the maturity spectrum of public and private securities should strengthen aggregate demand in the usual ways and thus help to end deflation. Of course, if operating in relatively short-dated Treasury debt proved insufficient, the Fed could also attempt to cap yields of Treasury securities at still longer maturities—say, three to six years. Yet another option would be for the Fed to use its existing authority to operate in the markets for agency debt (for example, mortgage-backed securities issued by Ginnie Mae, the Government National Mortgage Association).

Is it that Bernanke offered a clear warning to those planning on "shorting" Treasuries? When the Fed announced its plans to buy longer dated Treasuries, prices rallied and yields plummeted, but since then yields have rebounded and prices have fallen, forcing the Fed to buy more Treasuries. The jury is still out on whether Bernanke's long-held plans will meet with success. Bernanke explained in his speech that he has history on his side:

Historical experience tends to support the proposition that a sufficiently determined Fed can peg or cap Treasury bond prices and yields at other than the shortest maturities. The most striking episode of bond-price pegging occurred during the years before the Federal Reserve–Treasury Accord of 1951. Prior to that agreement, which freed the Fed from its responsibility to fix yields on government debt, the Fed maintained a ceiling of 2.5 percent on long-term Treasury bonds for nearly a decade. Moreover, it simultaneously established a ceiling on the 12-month Treasury certificate of between .875 percent and 1.25 percent and, during the first half of that period, a rate of .375 percent on 90-day Treasury bills. The Fed was able to achieve these low interest rates despite a level of outstanding government debt (relative to GDP) significantly greater than we have today, as well as inflation rates substantially more variable. At times, in order to enforce these low rates, the Fed actually had to purchase the bulk of outstanding 90-day bills. Interestingly, though, the Fed enforced the 2.5 percent ceiling on long-term bond yields for nearly a decade without ever holding a substantial share of outstanding long-maturity bonds. For example, the Fed held 7 percent of outstanding Treasury securities in 1945 and 9.2 percent in 1951 (the year of the accord), almost entirely in the form of 90-day bills. By comparison, in 2001 the Fed held 9.7 percent of the stock of outstanding Treasury debt.

Bernanke was confident in 2002. Does he remain so today? Thus far, he has stuck to his 2002 playbook. We'll soon know whether the central bank can defeat deflation or whether it will go too far and trigger sharper-than-expected inflation. The outcome will have a direct impact on metals prices, but it's not just tangible economic results that will tell the tale of the metals in the course of the next several years. The outcome also depends on whether regulators such as Bernanke can restore confidence in the financial markets.

SCENARIOS FOR COINS AND BULLION

The serious problems in both the United States and world economies continue to spur a flight of investors to gold and silver. Those investors are looking not only for a safe place to put some of their money but also for answers on what's next and what the potential scenarios are. Author and coin dealer Scott Travers sees two likely scenarios.

"One," he says, "would be further recession, accompanied initially by some deflation, but then by significant inflation—an economic climate which historically has triggered major price gains for coins and precious metals."

The other scenario, Travers says, may be less palatable to some of those holding gold: "The other would be a depression-like environment—but as strange as it may seem, that, too, would give coins a shot in the arm. People would spend much of that time on their hobbies, including coin collecting." Travers goes on to say that "although they wouldn't be buying million-dollar rarities, they'd be getting more deeply involved in the hobby—and eventually, when conditions improved, that interest would translate into greater market activity."

Economic problems abound in the world today, and one doesn't have to look too far to find disconcerting news. As recently as 2006 the thought that the United States might be headed toward a depression was debated only in the most wonky of economic circles. Now it's discussed everywhere, whether in the corporate boardroom, the local pizza shop, or on financial television. While panic hasn't hit the streets and there are no lines of anxious depositors at banks, shortages of goods, or societal disorder, there's enough concern about money and markets for investors to take notice and avoid risks after heavy losses in other assets. In increasing numbers, they're buying coins and metals.

And why not? Coins have been around for more than two thousand years as a medium of exchange, and jewelry has been worn for more than seven thousand years. Whether a new crop of powerful buyers chooses to marvel at the beauty of coin acquisitions or dispassionately spend hundreds of thousands—or even millions—of dollars for a position in precious metals is up to those investors. But one thing is certain: Silver, gold, and platinum have history on their side, with gold in particular having served as a store of substantial financial value for millennia. It's also abundantly clear that current demand is strong for gold and silver products and will remain so until the financial difficulties are resolved. And that could take years.

2

RUNNING WITH THE BULLS

Here's a rule that many learned the hard way in 2008: Stocks can most definitely go to a wealth-destroying $0, but not so with precious metals. Once discovered and extracted, metals retain intrinsic value, and it's virtually impossible for them to sink to $0. Metals have certainly seen their share of bear markets—there is no perfect investment play—but in the end, while companies can go belly-up and completely flatline, investors in gold, silver, and even copper are at least left with holdings that have intrinsic value and have been tradable for the last several thousand years.

The financial markets are mostly "What have you done for me lately?" kinds of places. Ten years ago, in late 1999, gold and silver were also-rans that had slogged through the previous decade at bottom-feeder levels—two hundred fifty dollars to three hundred dollars an ounce for gold, under five dollars for silver—following the wild early '80s, when precious metals had soared and then crashed and burned.

But a funny thing happened on the way to the twenty-first century. The dot-com boom busted, collapsing the stock market by 2002, and gold and silver, along with a variety of other hard asset investments, regained their luster. Stocks made a brief comeback and Wall Street rallied to scale record highs by the fall of 2006 but then came crashing back down in 2008, sending investors scurrying for safe-haven plays far from the pungent smell of financial death and destruction in the equities market.

A sense of fear and distrust now pervade the atmosphere "on the Street," and the question of which bank, brokerage house, or Ponzi investment scheme will explode next is nervously anticipated. Wall Street will never be the same. Even a positive event such as the more than 30 percent rally for the stock market from its March 2009 lows leaves all too many guessing whether a full-blown recovery is on the way, or whether stocks will pull back once again and mark lower lows.

The market collapse of 2008 is all to blame. Investors—save for the scant few who timed their investments perfectly—are waking up and realizing that the past decade has become a bad dream. Many can't help but feel that they were scammed by claims of wondrous investment performance from financial "experts" who touted equities as virtually outperforming every asset class under the sun.

STOCKS—A DECADE OF UNDERPERFORMANCE

The ten-year time frame is used frequently in this book since it's a popular benchmark that the mutual fund industry uses for gauging "long-term" performance of its key funds. Any way you look at it, the last decade has been a dreary one for stocks, perhaps drearier than what the fund and index benchmarks show. For buy-and-hold investors in funds that mimic the performance of indexes such as the S&P 500, the decade has been a disaster. The mantra of buy-and-hold success has largely been a myth, unless you've bought and held for at least twenty years and haven't made many bad investment timing decisions along the way.

But the financial partygoers continued to party even as storm clouds gathered, acting as if it was still 1999—the year the S&P soared above fourteen hundred. That figure seems nosebleed-high today, with the S&P languishing at nine hundred, but it was the source of sheer exhilaration in 1999—for in 1989, it had been a mere three hundred. The tailspin of recent years has left those partygoers with horrible hangovers and little to show unless they didn't have their investments on autopilot and were able to perfectly time tops and bottoms in the market. The reality has set in that the 2007 highs were merely failed retreads of the 1999 highs.

As one example, the Vanguard 500 Fund, with nearly $75 billion in assets, had a net negative performance of 1.46 percent per year over the last ten years—showing a clear, steady downturn prior to the 2008 crash. That may not sound like much, but the losses add up: A $10,000 investment in the benchmark fund in 1999 would have shrunk to $8,539.20 in 2009.

▪ VANGUARD 500 FUND AVERAGE ANNUAL PERFORMANCE

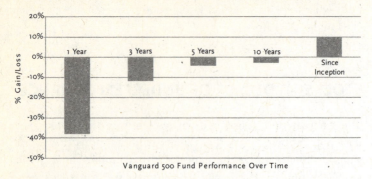

Vanguard 500 Fund Performance Over Time

No "Fun" in Funds. As long as the stock market continues to limp, so too will the performance of funds like the S&P 500 that mimic the performance of the biggest stocks around. The Vanguard 500 fund is not particularly worse or better than other funds of its ilk but with its brand name it stands out among the many wrecks on the investment superhighway. *Data source: Vanguard*

The Dow Jones Industrial Average (DJIA) has suffered a similar performance shortfall—down from nine thousand a decade ago to just eighty five hundred today.

The Dow, S&P 500, and other indexes have a highly effective way of enhancing their performance over time: As managed indexes, they can choose which companies are included in their data. When a company's shares die, or the company is taken over, its stock is purged from the indexes and replaced with a fresh—and presumably more robust—component. This has served to give the indices a better chance of being higher than if no changes had been made.

During 2008, more than forty changes were made to the S&P 500 and three replacements took place in the thirty-stock Dow Jones Industrial Average. In mid-2009 General Motors and Citigroup were booted from the Dow, and it's unclear at this writing whether other major underperformers will be removed as well.

For S&P the forty changes made to its S&P 500 index are considerable when S&P's own position on adding and deleting stocks is examined. Its published "S&P U.S. Indices Index Methodology" states:

Standard & Poor's believes turnover in index membership should be avoided when possible. At times a company may appear to temporarily violate one or more of the addition criteria. However, the addition criteria are for addition to an index, not for continued membership. As a result, an index constituent that appears to violate criteria for addition to that index will not be deleted unless ongoing conditions warrant an index change. When a company is removed from an index, Standard & Poor's will explain the basis for the removal.

S&P ended up having a very busy 2008 due to sudden and seismic shifts in the investment landscape.

DALBAR

For the last fifteen years an organization known as DALBAR Inc. has published its Quantitative Analysis of Investor Behavior (QAIB). It gauges not only market performance but investors' success in timing the market. Rigorous studies done by DALBAR show that stock market returns have been negative on an annualized basis over the past ten years, positive but paltry over the last twenty years, and that investors are their own worst enemy where timing the market is concerned.

The QAIB report's positive investor returns show up within the twenty-year time frame at an average annual rate for the S&P 500 of 8.3 percent. Within a ten-year time span the return is −1.5 percent annually through the end of 2008, −2.4 percent over five years, −8.7 percent over three years, and −37 percent for 2008.

Those return figures, while exactly reflecting the S&P 500, don't account for the average, real-world investor and how she or he might react to large fluctuations in market values. The DALBAR report offers a sobering conclusion that investor returns are more than likely worse than what the base-case S&P 500 benchmark suggests since investors are prone to be more wrong in their market timing decisions than right.

When fund inflow and outflows are taken into account, DALBAR notes, it is more likely that over a twenty-year period stock investors reaped gains of just 1.87 percent annually instead of a more than 8 percent annual rise recorded for the S&P 500 over that period.

In its concluding remarks, DALBAR makes a cogent suggestion: " . . . the same old renditions of 'stay the course' ring hollow and flat—unless they're supported by strategies that allow investors to rest easy during the turbulent times."

So the dirty little secret that really isn't a secret is out: Most who have participated in stock ownership through mutual funds that mimic the broad-based benchmark indexes have been fleeced with meager returns and even then for only the longest of long-term holders (twenty years or more).

SHORT-SHRIFTED IN STOCKS; GOLD RALLIES

With precious metals, the story has been dramatically different during the last decade. Metals have gained. And with these assets, there are no substitutions: gold is gold, silver is silver, and so forth.

While benchmark indexes have suffered, narrower gauges of market areas have done well, though off their highs of 2008. The PHLX (Philadelphia Stock Exchange) Gold/Silver Index has been a standout performer over the past decade. According to Nasdaqomxtrader.com, a NASDAQ-run Web site, the index is "designed to track the performance of a set of companies engaged in gold or silver mining sector."

GOLD SOARS OVER THE LAST DECADE

Gold emerged over the last decade not only as a safe-haven investment, but an investment that generated wealth, rising from three hundred dollars an ounce to more than nine hundred dollars. The long-term trend, even with the 1981 implosion, has been higher. When the United States was on a gold standard, the price of the metal remained highly stable until the late 1960s.

■ **AVERAGE GOLD PRICE 1900–2007**

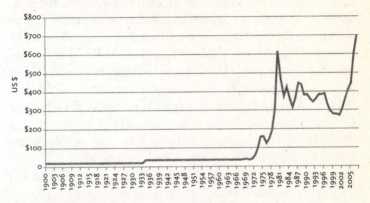

Average Gold Price 1900–2007. *Data source: World Gold Council (WGC)*

BULLISH FUNDAMENTALS FOR GOLD

Commodities' about-face wasn't completely bad news for traditional investment areas. Helping to offset the tarnish caused by world recession and deleveraging, central bank gold sales fell to a nine-year low of 357 metric tons (MT), which was well short of the five hundred-MT limit under the Central Bank Gold Agreement. Mining production is hovering at an eleven-year low at this writing, according to the World Gold Council. As gold prices leveled off from the $1,000+ high of early 2008, jewelry consumption rose 8 percent year after year, giving gold demand a lift of nearly 19 percent in the third quarter of 2008. According to Gold Council data, overall gold supply slid 10 percent.

CENTRAL BANK GOLD SALES CURTAILED

Central banks' diminished gold sales in recent years shouldn't have come as a complete surprise. Time and time again, world central banks found buyers all too willing to relieve them of their national treasure when they sold tons of gold during the 1990s, which suppressed the metal's price and diminished their return. They simply threw in the towel on further gold sales. The most egregious example of complete tomfoolery in central bank gold selling was the 1999 decision by the Bank of England to sell 58 percent of its gold. Gordon Brown, then chancellor of the exchequer (equivalent to the U.S. Treasury secretary) and now British prime minister, made the fateful decision at the low of the gold market, when gold was trading at $250 an ounce. The sale is estimated to have cost British taxpayers nearly $5 billion—money the United Kingdom could surely use now as it combats widespread banking problems. Since then, central bank gold sales have been muted. Brown earned the nickname "Golden Brown" for the ill-timed gold sales.

Central bank gold sales are likely to be limited through 2010, now that bankers have come to realize that gold could reemerge on the world stage as an international currency and—as Germany's Bundesbank has pointed out, "national gold reserves have a confidence-building and stability function."

THE AFTERBURNERS GO ON FOR SILVER

Silver has also fared well in the last decade, advancing from $5.80 per ounce to more than $13 per ounce. Following the 2008 commodities crash, silver has been able to regain its composure and remains solidly above 1999 levels.

■ AVERAGE SILVER PRICE 1990–2008

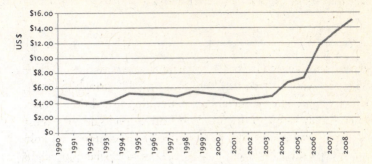

Average Silver Price 1990–2008. *Data source: COMEX*

DEMAND FOR SILVER IS STRONG

Through the U.S. Mint's American Eagle bullion coin program, more than 19.5 million ounces of silver were sold during 2008—an all-time high and an increase of 98 percent over 2007. The huge rise in silver bullion sales came even though the Mint suspended sales for a month and then rationed them. The dollar value of silver bullion sales topped a record $286 million, up 115 percent from 2007.

PLATINUM: THE BIGGER THEY ARE, THE HARDER THEY FALL

Platinum has been more complicated for investors. The precious metal shot to above two thousand dollars an ounce in June 2008 and crumbled to below the price of gold later in 2008: a spectacular crash and burn. Platinum's story is really about the automotive industry and its lessened need for the metal.

Platinum's chart, below, shows exceptional gains over the last decade, and no doubt as the automotive industry recovers, platinum is likely to show a strong rebound over the twelve hundred dollar level.

■ AVERAGE PLATINUM PRICE 1992–2009

Average Platinum Price 1992–2009. *Data source: COMEX*

GETTING DOWN TO BASE CASE

For metals such as copper, zinc, and nickel, the price performance has been more volatile, with the recent trading range far below the highs of 2008.

■ YEARLY NICKEL PRICE 1998–2009

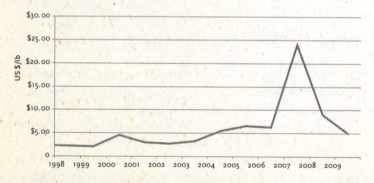

Yearly Nickel Price 1998–2009. Nickel, a key ingredient in stainless steel, batteries, and other industrial and commercial products, is likely to remain stuck at present price levels until the world economy improves. *Data source: Yearly closing nickel price for Kitco.com*

COMMODITIES' TEN-YEAR GAINS

As the old saying on Wall Street goes, "The trade works until it doesn't." The last decade was marked by a steady increase in demand for precious metals (as the gold and silver charts indicate), culminating in near-panic buying by early 2008 that drove gold above $1,030 per ounce and silver to above twenty dollars—a record high and multiyear high, respectively. By July 2008, relatively easy money had been made in commodities, whether metals, grains, or crude oil.

Then, as the world economy showed stark signs of slowing, metals (along with other commodities) tumbled from the highs of 2008 on the expectation that stunted economic growth would inhibit demand. Metals were also not immune to severe liquidation pressures by hedge funds, which faced sudden demand from customers looking for the return of their money.

But even after those recent setbacks, commodities remain above the levels of a decade ago. Corn, for example, rose to over $7.50 per bushel—and even though it fell substantially thereafter, it firmed up above four dollars, which is more than double its 1999 levels.

■ CORN PRICE 1999–2009

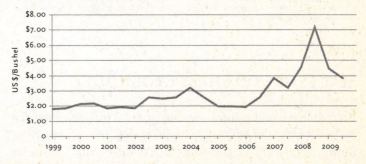

Corn Price 1999–2009. Why corn, in a book about coins? Growing numbers of analysts are keeping an eye on food-related futures, including corn, for clues on world crop output and whether adverse weather and political conditions might impact supply. If food shortages emerge, commodities investors say a boost in food prices could quickly propel gold even higher. *Data source: Chicago Board of Trade (CBOT)*

The same can be said for crude oil. While crude came close to soaring above $150 per barrel in 2008, its fall back to earth has stopped well short of its 1999 trading range of thirty dollars per barrel and could be headed to one hundred dollars a barrel in 2010 if inflation rears its ugly head enough.

■ AVERAGE WTI CRUDE PRICE 1967–2009

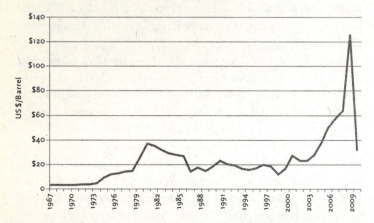

Crude Makes the World Go Round. If corn is being watched by some for clues on pricing pressure, then crude oil most assuredly is being tracked by many more analysts. The price of West Texas Intermediate (WTI) crude has suffered with the rest of the commodities world, but disruption threats remain to world supply. Gold has decoupled from crude recently—rising even as crude has fallen. However, any spike in crude is likely to present a stronger buying opportunity to gold investors. *Data source: CME Group*

REAL ESTATE ON SHAKY GROUND

It's common—and painful—knowledge that real estate has endured a spectacular bust following an equally spectacular boom. But this doesn't hold true over the very long term. Those who bought houses thirty years ago are still holding on to significant gains, according to both government data and Case-Schiller figures.

An especially troubling aspect of real estate, as of this writing, continues to be inventory, which remains tremendously bloated (more than a year's supply of homes for sale), exerting downward pressure on prices. Worse yet is the trouble the Federal Reserve is having as it struggles to keep mortgage rates under control. The long-term funding needs of the Treasury and the expansion of the Fed's balance sheet to take on risky bank assets have posed almost insuperable challenges for federal policymakers. The real estate outlook remains bleak as more interest rate resets are due to occur on adjustable-rate mortgages (ARMs) in 2010 and 2011.

BONDS MAKE THE GRADE

Savvy Treasury bond investors were rewarded in 2008 with returns of more than 10 percent, thanks to a rise in the ten-year price as yields fell in response to Fed rate cuts. Through 2009, bonds were standout outperformers, based on price levels over the last decade. The Bernanke playbook may make government purchases of longer-dated Treasuries inevitable, bringing further gains in price and even lower yields.

■ 10-YEAR TREASURY YIELD

10-Year Treasury Yield. *Data source: Daily closing 10-year Treasury yield*

THE ART MARKET

While art is not a mass consumer market where millions of units are available, as they are with coins and bullion, the price trends of the art market have been similar to those in collectible coins. The high end has seen price declines and lower-end activity hasn't taken up enough of the slack. Of course, for the super-wealthy, the fine collectibles market—ranging from multimillion-dollar paintings to authentic works by Tiffany to diamonds and emeralds—has continued to see demand. For the moderately wealthy who may have parted quickly with several hundred thousand dollars for a Warhol print, the times have been tough and have had a decidedly adverse impact on auction houses. Sotheby's and Christie's International both have imposed deep job cuts. The already disappointing year ended in a thud for both auction houses as 2008 drew to a close, with less than 70 percent of their inventory reportedly having been sold at end-of-year contemporary auctions.

The art market has become so severely hampered that Standard & Poor's has warned that it may reduce Sotheby's credit rating to junk status, saying the 265-year-old company's revenue will "decline substantially over the near term."

Profit margins and revenue have tumbled at major auction houses. These charts are perhaps the best method of gauging the condition of the art and collectibles markets, portraying a huge slide in revenue from auction activity.

For those who bought wheat at more than twelve dollars per bushel, or crude oil at $145, there's little to celebrate. Misery loves company, and whether one bought stocks at the peak, or wheat, or art, that misery abounds and the losses are painful. However for metals investors the picture is akin to "running with the bulls" as gold floats near one thousand dollars per ounce, along with strong price action for silver and platinum and a firming up for copper.

3

MAKING THE GRADE: TRENDS IN COIN GRADING

At its most basic level, coin grading is a system of number grades from 1 to 70. The lowest grade, 1, is a barely recognizable coin, while 70 is perfection. The system was set into place in 1977 by the American Numismatic Association (ANA), the world's largest organization of coin collectors.

It's beyond the scope of this book to go into great detail about the qualifications coin graders use to designate a coin. But several assessments are made. The grader will carefully examine the degree of wear, if any, the coin has experienced. Imperfections like scratches and nicks are examined. The strength of the strike of the coin when it was made is also assessed. In the end the coin grader also subjectively examines the coin's eye appeal (attractiveness) and its luster, or how it reflects light.

There are subdivisions of grades across the 1 to 70 scale. Grades 60 to 70, known as Mint State 60 through 70 (MS-60 through MS-70), represent coins that were never circulated and are in a pristine state of preservation. It is at these top levels of preservation where the biggest and most important coin transactions take place in the coin market. Accuracy in coin grading is critical at all levels of the scale and especially so in the active Mint State portion of the grading scale where transactions in the hundreds of thousands and even millions of dollars are taking place.

Big differences exist within the eleven grades of MS-60 to MS-70 designations:

MS-60: Represents a coin that just barely makes it into the uncirculated category. While it hasn't been passed from one hand to another, an MS-60 coin often has many scratches, nicks, and even gashes from rubbing against other coins in a bag of uncirculated coins. The same can be said for MS-63 coins, although in this higher grade, the bag marks are less apparent.

MS-65: A minor blemish may be the only thing that holds an MS-65 coin from a higher grade. At this point on the scale, eye appeal is highly desirable because of only minor flaws on the coin's surface.

MS-67: A coin at this grade would seem perfect to the naked eye, but under 5x magnification some minor flaws would become apparent to keep the coin from grading at the top levels of the scale.

MS-68, MS-69, MS-70: Highly sought after, but tough grades to win from the grading services. Scott Travers, author of *The Coin Collector's Survival Manual*, says, "The MS-70 grade is really more of a theoretical grade, a utopian goal that is constantly pursued but seldom attained." Likewise with MS-68 and MS-69, Travers says the grades are "attainable but only with great difficulty since the coins must be free of all but tiniest of flaws."

Farther below on the scale is the AU (About Uncirculated) part of the grading scale, from 50 to 59—so close to Mint State preservation, yet so far. These are still desirable coins with strong features, but the coins have been passed from hand to hand so that wear is apparent. Some of the coins in this population were once Mint State and far more valuable, but through careless handling that blemished the high points of the coin's surface were relegated to AU condition. The ramifications of such careless handling can be costly. For example, an MS-65 coin may be worth several thousand dollars at that grade level, but when it's handled and rubbed enough to show even slight wear, the coin may only be worth a few hundred dollars in AU-58 condition.

Below AU is the Extremely Fine (EF) designation: EF-40 and EF-45 coins that show more wear to a coin's high points.

Very Fine (VF-20 and VF-30) are coins that show considerable wear, but maintain fairly sharp major features.

Fine (F-12) are coins that show a strong degree of even wear with primary features that remain identifiable.

Very Good (VG-8) is not really all that good. At a level of 8, the coin has been worn to point of flat surfaces, though the design remains discernable.

Good (G-4) designations on the coin become faint, but somewhat discernable at this level of preservation.

About Good (AG-3) is a coin that is worn and smooth with an outline that barely shows the original design of the coin. However, sometimes collectors will buy this type of coin when examples are extremely rare and scarce.

A variety of coin-grading services are in operation, but two dominate the landscape and are widely considered the most reputable: the Professional Coin Grading Service (PCGS) and the Numismatic Guaranty Corporation (NGC). For a fee, coin collectors are invited by both services to submit their coins for grading.

Since accuracy of grading is crucial in the active, multimillion-dollar coin marketplace, a service was created in 2007 to judge the accuracy of graded coins: the Certified Acceptance Corporation, or CAC. While not a grading service, CAC verifies the authenticity of graded coins and verifies the grades themselves. CAC looks at a coin from the perspective of whether the coin grade reflects an A type coin, a coin that is high-end for the grade; a B type, which is average for the grade; or a C type, which is a coin that may, for example, be just barely worthy of a certain grade or is a coin of low-end quality for the grade. Whether this will force coin grading companies to introduce decimal grades (e.g., MS-65.2) remains to be seen.

A key concern in the coin industry is something known as "grade-flation," a (real or perceived) loosening of coin-grading standards over time, enabling some coins to attain a higher grade than deserved. The work of CAC is in part to combat this trend. In the words of John Albanese, founder of CAC and cofounder of PCGS, "the little sticker makes a big difference." CAC places a small oval sticker on the front of a certified coin holder to denote the coin meets stringent quality standards.

I asked Mr. Albanese some questions about CAC in light of what's at stake in the coin market and the state of coin grading.

J.K.: John, what's been going on in the coin grading business that led to creation of CAC?

Albanese: If I can give an analogy. If you go back a few years ago, hypothetically, if you bought a bond fund paying 8 percent, carrying investment-grade bonds, in that fund there may have been GM and GE. [Author's note: GM has since declared bankruptcy, while GE has taken billions of dollars in charges due to toxic assets on balance sheet.] They're both large companies, iconic companies. In our industry the difference between a low-end 65 and a high-end 65 is basically the same, very similar to the differences in GM and GE. One coin can be worth twice as much as the other, just like one bond could be worth twice as much as another. Unfortunately everything was being lumped together.

It got to the point where collectors and investors started getting smarter. They started reading articles on the Internet, participating in auctions. As they got smarter they said, hey there's a difference between a GE and GM, they're not all the same. And there's a difference in a low-end and a high-end MS-65, so therefore the gap started to widen so the higher-end MS-65—let's say the higher a coin, or B+ coin in some cases—had a 50 percent or 100 percent disparity with the 65-C coin.

All my life I've been selecting nicer coins and I found that the dealers and the collectors that were focusing on nice coins— high-end or investment-quality coins—were being punished, because their potential customers were comparing their price data to the lower-end coin. My coin had to compete with a lower-end [coin]; therefore, it was the tail wagging the dog. I compare it to a death spiral as the low-end coin was the focus of the market for sight-unseen trading on all the networks, and if someone had a bid of thirteen thousand dollars on a bust quarter obviously they're going to buy a low-end coin, they're not going to buy a high-end coin.

It was really the low-end coin dragging down the whole market and taking the high coins with them. I think what has happened since CAC's inception in late 2007 is that we have seen larger spread in coins because we have formalized the existence of the higher-end coin. Of course it is somewhat of a divisive business here; however, at least finally the people with a good eye paid a premium for nice coins—they're finally no longer being punished and are being rewarded for being fussy as opposed to having to compare their coins to a bottom-feeder.

CAC is fighting back. It's not a defensive move; it's an offensive move against grade-flation but also an offensive move against letting the GM bond dictate the whole bond market. Just like a high-end coin should perform better than a low-end coin.

I have nothing against low-end coins, I think it's okay to buy that bust quarter for twelve thousand dollars, but what was happening in our industry was that a lot of unsuspecting buyers were buying the low-end coin because of the label and paying the high-end price.

J.K.: This is obviously great for coin purchasers. How have the coin-grading services taken the arrival of CAC?

Albanese: I think it's a mixed bag. I think they realize every coin is different—just like every snowflake is different, every MS-65 is different.

J.K.: Why doesn't CAC just start its own grading service?

Albanese: The main answer is that we'd have the same dilemma. If a coin came—that bust quarter came in and it was a MS-65-C, but a real 65, we would still have to call it 65 to be numismatically correct. We couldn't call it a 64; it would be incorrect. We'd have the same dilemma. The C coin is really the dilemma. Of course some coins are over-graded and that's a whole other story. I think the issue is that the consumer, the investor, has gotten much more sophisticated—they're learning or seeking professional help. Twenty or thirty years ago when I started in the business the dealers controlled everything. I had people come in to me in the early days and say, "John, here's one hundred thousand dollars, get me something." Now it's more specific things—they'll want a silver dollar and want it to look a certain way. The client has gotten much smarter. CAC is just adapting to today's discriminating client.

J.K.: Is that a function of coins being seen by a broader segment of the population as asset class?

Albanese: A lot of new people are coming in. I believe coins are an emerging potential asset class. I don't think they're quite there yet. It's certainly emerging. I would challenge anyone to find me a collectible comparing to coins with the same amount of liquidity and transparency. If you went into an art gallery in New York City and bought a painting for fifty thousand dollars and brought it down the street and tried to sell it for half, my guess is that they would laugh at you. As much as people complain [about coin market spreads], coin markets with spreads being 18 to 30 percent, maybe that's high compared to stocks and bonds, but compared to other collectibles, [the spreads] are very much on the low end. I think of the antique and art trade and many of these paintings that sell at auction, three months later I see them in an advertisement for triple the price. You can call coins an asset class or a collectible; they certainly are much more liquid than other collectibles.

J.K.: How many coins have CAC stickered?

Albanese: I'm going to guess we've seen eighty thousand coins and 39 percent have stickered. The average coin submitted to us is in the six thousand to seven thousand dollar range, so it's been the higher-end coin.

J.K.: Which grading services do you sticker?

Albanese: At the moment PCGS- and NGC-slabbed coins. We hope to expand it in the future.

J.K.: How long will it take to even out grade-flation?

Albanese: At first, from what I've been told, the services, with just the rumor we were going to start, were a little tougher. I can't mention the service, but in the last few months, it seems they've gone the other way where lots of Morgan dollars in MS-65 or -66, mostly the common to semi-common dates from a few hundred dollars to a few thousand dollars, they've gotten extremely liberal. I've seen a lot of coins all of the sudden graded 65 that I grade 63, so I think in this case on silvers they threw in the towel on grade-flation. I don't know what happened—maybe they changed graders.

I think another problem is that maybe 20 percent of the coins that come out of services are maybe C coins. I think what's happened because of the constant cherry-picking by collectors and dealers, is that C-coin seems to linger on the market. What you see on the market is the low-end that has accumulated for maybe even decades and those coins don't come off the market as fast as the A or B coin. The A or B coins disappear into collections quite rapidly. So the C coin is left lingering. If you went to a coin show and looked around at coins, if you have an experienced eye, you would say, "Boy, this is pretty scary," but it's really an accumulation of twenty years of coins. Where I think, if you were sitting at the grading service looking at what was coming out of the plant every day, you [would] say, "Hey, these coins are fine." Overall you can live with it.

Unfortunately, the remnants end up on the market and those, of course, drag the market down because the prices keep getting cheaper and cheaper until those C coins go away. It's very similar to the mortgage market: You have your subprime mortgages and you have your subprime coins. The subprime coins in a weak market or even a level or correcting market, there are very few bidders and they get crushed. In a lot of cases like the bust quarter, which I think is an exaggeration of the market, but where a 65-C coin in a lot of cases is bringing the price of a 64-B coin. It's getting to the point where if you're a crack-out dealer and you see a nice 64 bust quarter, and say it's eleven thousand dollars, if I get into a 65 I only make 10 percent.

So I believe if the current trends continue it could put a severe cramp on the crack-out dealers and the grading services because it won't pay to upgrade a coin, because who wants a C coin?

J.K.: Is it an automatic given that if you have, for example, an old slabbed PCGS coin that it's a one-point upgrade, or do you need to have the eye?

Albanese: You have to have the eye. If you speak to some dealers they'll say, "Hey by the way, if the coin has been in a holder for twenty years and hasn't been cracked out yet, there's a reason." Some of them are off-the-charts terrible and there's a reason why they're in an old holder. For some coins, it doesn't pay to crack them out. You have a silver commemorative like a Wisconsin, or a New York, or Roanoke and you can crack it out from a 65 to 66 holder, it's only a ten dollar difference in price. So why pay twenty dollars to crack it out? In some coins the spreads are so narrow that it doesn't pay. Obviously on certain coins it does pay; they call them the spread coins. An 1891-O silver dollar is a coin that can go from seven hundred dollars in 64 to a seven thousand dollar in 65, [so there's] a very big temptation to get that coin into a higher graded holder. Some coins, like maybe the 1880-CC [or] 1881-CC, might go from seven hundred dollars to a thousand dollars, not as much of a spread—if you want to call it arbitrage, why bother? But the 1891-O, they're going to try that coin and try that coin.

J.K.: Let's talk about your CAC stickers.

Albanese: The gold sticker is hardly ever used. Out of eighty thousand coins or so, we've done about 150 gold stickers. So were talking about almost about two out of a thousand. It's been very low and the reason is simply consumer protection. When grading standards were extremely strict in the late 1980s or early '90s, a proof Morgan dollar may have been graded at the time at 66. That comes in today and we look at it and say, "Wow, this is a nice 67," not even maybe it's a 67, maybe it's not—it's by far an MS-67. We're talking about a point-and-a-half difference. In that case we give a gold sticker. It's really to notify the consumer by saying don't sell this coin at this slabbed grade, sell at the next-highest grade; if you sell at that [lower] grade, you're doing yourself a disservice. It's really to alert the consumer that he should get his coin regraded. Many times those coins trade and many times those coins trade at the next-highest grade anyway. Don't whip out a Greysheet and sell it at bid.

J.K.: Have there been any groups of coins inaccurately graded by the services?

Albanese: The biggest difference at CAC to what is coming out of the plant, the services, is Saint-Gaudens twenty-dollar gold pieces in 65 and 66. We think they're getting graded too high. That's a philosophical difference. Obviously they think they're right, and we think we're right, and that's not going to change.

J.K.: Are those gold pieces trading so actively in the market over-graded?

Albanese: In my opinion they're over-graded. It's an opinion: In my opinion, over-graded; in their opinion, they're graded fine.

J.K.: There's a lot at stake financially amid these opinions—

Albanese: We make markets in our coins. In just a little over a year we've done about $80 to $85 million in volume. We make markets, we have a lot of capital, we put our money on the line when we grade coins. We're not going to be relaxed because we know if we do a bad job we'll end up owning all of the coins. So far it's been very even—despite the shocks in the stock market, we've had very, very fluid markets. I can't keep enough coins in stock.

J.K.: CAC's emergence came at quite an interesting time where stocks and other assets were collapsing, yet coins were moving higher.

Albanese: Probably luck in that case. I was thinking about CAC about three years before we even started it. It was just a matter of time to have the business plan developed and the software. In reality coins have done very well.

You have to remember as the stock market declined and the real-estate market declined, certain coins have actually declined too. Some coins are tied to the wealth effect and that might be very high-end collector coins. You have collectors and investors and hoarders. Right now you have a lot of hoarders—people are panicked. A lot of hot money is going to gold. The hot money can exit quickly. If you're an average collector and your house was worth $600,000 and now it's worth $480,000 and your IRA, Keogh, or 401(k) is down 40 percent, you're going to be less inclined to pull the trigger on a two-cent piece at ten thousand dollars. I think in order to buy a two-cent piece for ten thousand dollars you have to feel pretty good about prospects of your career and your other investments holdings, and when you see this kind of market we have now, more than likely if that collector is going to buy anything at all, he's going to buy gold, forget the two-cent piece—that can wait. A lot of collector coins have suffered a little bit; we're softer here. Although the coins that are considered investment coins, like silver coins, like silver dollars, or gold coins, especially, have done well.

J.K.: Have the gold buyers gone overboard; are they betting against the United States, are they betting against the government, the present administration?

Albanese: I was speaking to a gentleman the other day who is a hard-money guy. He said, "John, if you were in that raft from the *Titanic,* or had a life vest after it sunk, would you sell your life vest for a thousand dollars?" Of course you wouldn't. Are they betting against government? I don't know. I have life insurance. I hope it isn't used in the near term. I know it will be used one day. I have fire insurance. Am I hoping for a fire? No, of course not. Am I hoping I die so my wife can collect? Of course not. Maybe a percentage of your assets in gold as a hedge, I can understand that. I tell people, listen I'm not an investment counselor, but put a few percentage points of your assets in coins, or gold, and hope it goes down. That's what I tell them. There are some people who have most of their assets in gold and I do know some of those people. They do hope and do wish that Obama fails and the government fails and there's hyperinflation and chaos in the streets and martial law; they do hope that they'll have all the money, and they're sort of miserly. I do believe they're betting against the United States. I hope they're wrong. The guy with the $600,000 house and the two-cent piece set, if he has twenty Krugerrands stashed for emergency—you have some bottled water, a can of tuna fish, what's wrong with that? You hope you don't need to use it.

J.K.: There are doom-and-gloom silver people as well— they think buying Morgan dollars is a good idea.

Albanese: I believe that and I see it in every cycle. If gold were to double to eighteen hundred dollars, my guess is that silver would triple or quadruple. It's a higher beta, it's like buying a cheap stock versus a hundred dollar stock. The cheap stocks in a bull market will outpace them percentage-wise; now when the market comes down, of course, they collapse. Now the silver market is a lot more volatile; I think the average guy can walk in—which they're doing like crazy—walk into a coin shop and buy a silver dollar, buy a one-ounce bar, buy a ten-ounce bar. Of course to the doomsday-ers, if gold is five thousand dollars and you want to go to a grocery store, well you're not going to bring a Krugerrand to buy a meatloaf—you're going to bring maybe a silver dollar, or a silver quarter. You're not going to fill up your tank with an ounce of gold; maybe you'll buy a car with five ounces of gold. They want to have something in smaller denominations—that's why they choose silver. I remember even back in Y2K, even [in the] 1980s, everyone wanted silver dimes—they wanted small denominations, something small to buy groceries with. Let's just say, I think they're wrong; I hope they're wrong.

J.K.: The CAC network is growing—

Albanese: CAC dealers love our coins and are doing very well. I believe the CAC dealers are capturing a larger share of the market share—[it's a] shrinking marketplace, but we're getting a bigger share. The non-CAC dealers don't like us because they don't have our product. It's clear to me that many coin dealers know how to grade and many don't. Just because a coin may look nice to you, we can technically show why it might not be nice. We're not talking about costume jewelry here, where your wife might pick out a necklace that looks beautiful. Well, some coins look beautiful but they may, on closer inspection, be flawed.

In consideration of the comments of John Albanese, it was decided to get a reaction to Albanese's CAC verification service from one of the major coin-grading services. Mark Salzberg, chairman of the NGC, rose to the task.

J.K.: What do you think of CAC?

Mark Salzberg: I know John Albanese very well—we grew up together. He is stickering coins he likes and that are theoretically solid for the grade. If he continues to do that he will sticker more and more NGC coins. He's done a nice job of building that, trading that kind of work. He calls it a verification service, it's not, certainly, a grading service, but it verifies, in his opinion, that the coin is solid for the grade. He also makes a market in that so I believe it has helped NGC. It's a different type of model, which is unique and I don't see it in other markets, but the collectibles market has different fundamentals than the financial markets.

J.K.: What about the plethora of grading services out there beyond PCGS and the CAC verification service. What do you think of the smaller grading services?

Salzberg: These third-world grading services are a disaster—they should just go away. There's no redeeming quality to them. They've demonstrated they do more harm than good. Ninety-five percent of the coins sold in auction or on the bourse floor are NGC or PCGS, the prices realized are largely in parity, that's a fact that speaks volumes. The market is saying the only use for these third-world grading services is for coins that don't work at NGC or PCGS. You find counterfeits, misattributed things, you find obviously over-graded coins and the holders themselves are a disaster. And that's only the next two or three grading services. If you go below that they're criminal.

J.K.: Has grading in general been an evolutionary type of process? Has there been a refinement in the attitude toward how a coin is graded and what grade it deserves?

Salzberg: Grading is an art and not a science. You have a learning curve. If you look at it from when NGC was first opened and John Albanese and I were grading, we, for example, would get in an early ten dollar gold piece—a perfect example was a 1795 ten dollar, from a famous collection. Now that coin came in and we graded it at MS-65, which was an extraordinarily high grade. But at the time we both thought it was a gem and we both had not seen another one that had came close. So in our minds at the time it was a 65. As the years have gone by, I've graded personally millions of coins and have see dozens of 1795 uncirculated ten dollars, I now easily would grade that coin a MS-67 because you have a frame of reference and a learning curve. Back then there were a handful of people in the country that got to see that coin. So how would you possibly know compared to other 1795 ten dollars how that coin ranks? Now we know it's the finest, now we know you have to be a little lenient on early gold. You [could] call that grade-flation or a learning curve—I call that a learning curve.

Now in some areas there's been tweaking—we call it a glacial effect on grading and that is based on what I hear in the marketplace and what, in general, the market is saying, for example, there are the 1923-D gold pieces, which come very flashy. So if you grade that coin a little bit different from a 1924 and you could accept a few more marks, but they come with great color and they're flashy, that coin as a 1924 would grade as MS-64, the 1923-D is probably more acceptable as an MS-65. So there are little tweaks here and there and I think it's an evolutionary process—there is a learning curve.

We've graded about 17 million coins at this point; there's a lot of nuances to grading coins, especially federal coinage from 1792 to date, in every mint, every metal, and every denomination—there are millions of combinations. Internally we could probably grade by tenths of a point because we're speaking that language. It's basically a language you're trying to communicate when you're grading a coin. There are some subtleties and we've been accused of grade-flation. Well, there's been a minor amount of that, but I think the majority of it is a learning curve.

J.K.: What about coins that are slabbed in older holders from, say, a decade or more ago? Are they candidates for automatic upgrades?

Salzberg: It's funny you should ask that. I was recently at a Baltimore coin show and a guy came up to me and said he submitted five coins and every coin came back the same grade [as was previously given]. He said we were tight. I said, "How am I tight if every coin came back the same grade that came out of our holders?" He said it came from an old-time collection that was over fifteen years old. I said the grading was accurate. Why does it necessarily have to be that they went up in grade because we graded them fifteen years ago? On the other hand, someone showed me some coins that were graded in 1988 when more darkly and thicker toned [coins] were more acceptable as an MS-65; those coins today are less acceptable on the marketplace because of very heavy toning. So you could make a case that some of those coins should be graded *lower* [emphasis added].

I think that grading is such a subjective thing that if you took the top twenty graders in the country and you put us in a room together we could probably all agree pretty much, or be very close. But if you go down to the next fifty, you're going to have a spread there of about a point. When people tell you these generalities, I don't buy into it.

We've introduced a new holder that's coated and scratch resistant. There's a perception that holders scratch, which affects the optic quality and so you see the coin in a different light; it looks like the coin is not the quality that the label might say. Recently John Albanese had sent a coin in for reholdering. He sent it to me, and I sent it back to him. He said, "Wow, it looks great." And I said that's our new holder. There's no scratching, [so the coins are] optically perfect and [they] look fantastic. So if you go through a dealer's inventory he banged around for several months, the coins aren't going to look as good. They get reholdered and that grading looks great.

J.K.: How tough of a daily slog is it between the grading services, including with your largest competitor, PCGS?

Salzberg: I look at NGC from a very simple point of view. We have the least amount of conflicts of interest. We haven't changed our business model since the founding of NGC and that is to be impartial, to be arm's length, to try to acquire the best talent, the best experts in the world, and bring them under our roof. I don't have to, on a daily basis, worry about whether I'm going to be selling coins. I don't have to worry about who owns the coins. I don't have to worry about my checkbook. Basically my job is to grade coins accurately and consistently. If you step out of the model then you have conflicts.

Yeah, you could say there's a competition. PCGS has a different model than we do. They have a very good brand, they have a registry that's exclusive to PCGS. In my opinion we're more numismatists here. Every one of the experts I have on staff was a success out in the marketplace for the most part before coming on to NGC on a full-time basis. I would say we've done very well just taking the high road and bolting on different services such as NCS Conservation, which conserves the national collection. We've done a hell of a job running a good business and being an international presence, being profitable, and sticking to areas that we know.

J.K.: How is the recession impacting NGC?

Salzberg: Actually surprisingly well. The areas that I would say were hit the most were the modern coin section, however that's been more than replaced by the generic gold [and] general bullion-related items; and vintage coins have been very strong. The other thing about our business is that we're very diversified because we're worldwide at this point. We have deals in China, Singapore, Europe, and so world markets is our fastest-growing segment of submissions at the moment. I would say very, very—we're weathering this very nicely.

J.K.: How does NGC guard against counterfeit holders that might come out of China? I know that there have been some phony PCGS holders from out of China.

Salzberg: We just recently introduced our next-generation holder, which I think is the best on the market. It's hermetically sealed, it has a bar code that is anti-counterfeit—the best that has ever been seen. I think the hologram is really the most difficult thing to counterfeit. Our holder has extraordinary anti-counterfeiting measures. The label itself has a metallic strip on it embedded "NGC" all over the place; the hologram is state of the art, so we're way ahead of that. We're also imaging every single coin that comes through NGC, so the last million or so coins that we've graded are in a database where the individual can go and log on and actually confirm that what they're holding is the coin that they've graded by going to our database. We're definitely way ahead of the curve on that.

There had been a couple of coins that were advertised on eBay as being NGC graded, they were so primitive and obvious; they were bust dollars that were graded Extra Fine. The holder and the coin were counterfeit. It's very obvious it's primitive where we consider it something that we've guarded against, and we've done a good job of that.

J.K.: Are you surprised by the strong ten-year performance of gold, which has more than tripled, versus a loss for stocks?

Salzberg: My observations are that gold is a safe haven at the moment and at the same time it's a hedge against inflation. What I've noticed in addition to that is that people want the physical gold. They're buying whatever they can get their hands on—whether it's Krugerrands, or Maple Leafs, or circulated twenty dollar gold pieces. Some others are buying graded U.S. gold twenty dollars, et cetera.

I get asked this question often: "What should I do? Should I buy gold?" My suggestion is if you're going to buy gold, buy physical gold, but don't pay the huge premiums that exist—try to pay the least amount of premium because historically circulated twenty-libs [Liberty Head twenty dollar gold coins], or Saints [Saint-Gaudens twenty dollar gold coins] have gone to 10 percent to 15 percent over melt and now they're bringing 30 to 40 percent over melt because there is such a demand over physical. The reason there is such demand for the physical is that people simply don't trust the ETFs [exchange-traded funds] or paper. You can buy GLD on the stock exchange, but people have said, I'm not going to buy stock because (a) I'm not sure it's going to be there, or (b) [it could] be confiscated. Those are the question and comments I've gotten.

It's really been a very powerful influx in the coin business and, I think, doesn't surprise me that gold over the long run has done fairly well considering that countries are leaping over each other to debase their currency, or printing money every day. Gold as you see it in the ads has never been worth zero and it doesn't disappear. General vintage U.S. coins and better-quality numismatic items also have a positive effect from this because of the migration and up-selling of individuals who are buying bullion today, who never thought about buying a coin, but then will eventually migrate into better and maybe better items and then get into type coins—the general theme of the American public and, in general, the world now is that maybe part of a portfolio should be in hard assets and maybe there should be gold or silver or platinum, and they're advised to buy coins. If you take a small percentage of that—the new influx of funds coming into bullion, you can see how this has influenced rare coins dramatically. Obviously these are finite material and the finer items have been doing very well.

J.K.: In the grand scheme of things, is gold over-owned, or under-owned relative to other assets?

Salzberg: In general it has been under-owned. You can see the bias even in an unbiased newspaper like the *Wall Street Journal*—they take every opportunity to sort of dis gold and be negative about gold and owning gold because, let's face it, their publication is about stocks and I think in general it's time to maintain your capital, maintain your assets and one way to do it is diversification. The whole "diversified in stocks only," or bonds only, is gone out the window in my opinion. I'm not a financial planner [but] I can still see the trend toward gold, and from my small amount of knowledge that I have in this area the debt we incur in this country on a weekly basis, or a monthly basis, dwarfs that amount of gold that's aboveground. At some point if people lose faith in the dollar, gold is going to look very, very cheap. I'm not an economist, but this is the average guy talking. The smart guys who are buying really valuable coins and others who have come into this market that are associated with the stock market are trying to get their money out of equities and into hard assets like gold and better coins.

J.K.: What about the new collector who wants some gold on hand? Is it better to buy an unslabbed Gold Eagle, or should they buy an MS-70 graded Gold Eagle?

Salzberg: I would look at it more as, "should a person buy a Gold Eagle in 69, or an ungraded Gold Eagle?" because they're probably one and the same. I would prefer the graded 69 because they don't bring the premium—they're graded, they're protected. And I think there's a ready market for both items ungraded and graded, but there's just a little bit more of an assurance with the slabbed coin that the coin is more of a decent quality. MS-70? Seventy is more of a collectors' item. If there's too much of a premium over 69

I wouldn't recommend a 70; however, there is a reality out there and the reality is, you go on eBay or a public auction and these better bullion coins in 70 are bringing very good money. There's a lot of collector base for the 70s. A hundred years ago, people thought gold pieces were common and not worthy of collecting. Well, a hundred years from now, or fifty years from now, these coins are going to be considered fairly scarce, probably. So it's depending on how you look at it and your horizon.

We've developed a product here which is called the Certified Bullion product. We're not going to be grading the coin, but we're going to be certifying an Eagle of its content and weight and that it is an American Eagle. The reason we're doing that is because there have been counterfeit platinum coins that have come through. It's not a prevalent problem but when you take a novice who's getting into this, they don't have a clue if the coin is authentic, so we give an extra bit of assurance that the coin has been certified by NGC for weight and content. We don't make any money on it, we holder these coins at a very reduced rate and larger sellers can easily sell these kinds of coins with our new product, which puts a certified product into the hands of the customer.

J.K.: What has been most impacted by the recession in the modern coins area?

Salzberg: It's more of the modern proof sets. We're seeing less and less of that. In general, it's just a slowdown across the board in modern—there's less being sold on television, less being sold on eBay. When oil was at $140 [a barrel] that had a noticeable effect. The person who is going to buy a fifty dollar or hundred dollar modern coin is the same person who is going to think twice about doing that if he's got to fill his gas tank, but that market was more than offset by the demand for gold and the general health of the vintage market.

J.K.: What has been standout in the vintage market?

Salzberg: Really superb items, and I think you can really say this across all categories of collectibles—things that are just standout where people say, "Wow." Those are the type of coins that have held their value, or have gone down the least. These are the type of items that we can learn from. Personally, I've always collected the very, very finest that I can afford—great eye appeal, great originality, and rarity. I've felt good about owning those because they are desirable across all categories. The people who can buy those coins haven't been as affected by the recent downturn.

The more common, better date items—93s dollars, 32s quarters in circ—those are the items that have gotten hurt a little bit more. The more common items have taken the biggest beating. We're not talking anything even close to what the stock market got hit with, but 20 percent drops in some of the more common vintage coins. But you can make an argument that some of the real vintage standouts have really held their own: at the most, 10 percent down from their highs.

J.K.: What were early warning indicators that swung in favor of coins?

Salzberg: I'm fortunate to be in an industry and a position where I meet some very sophisticated individuals across all categories—there are hedge fund managers, wealthy individuals, CEOs that collect coins. You could see the behavior change in these individuals probably two years ago. Many of them said, "I'm getting my money out of equities, things have just become too historically overvalued." They started to buy more rare coins and things with historic values, the best they could afford. They said they would put those purchases away in an effort to exit out of equities and get out of hard assets. You saw this from literally two years ago. All of them have said the velocity of this downturn is what surprised them the most and some of them got caught in the downdraft of the last three or four months and didn't completely convert and still lost quite a bit of money. They were right, but a little slow to do it.

4

THE KINGSLAND COLLECTIBLES INDICES

In combing through the data for this book, the author has come to realize that gauges of information on collectibles and assets are not readily available. Google searches come up with bits and pieces of data; in this day and age there ought to be an easier way to get the pulse on markets outside the traditional financial markets universe.

Here in chapter 4, the Kingsland Collectibles Indices, created through a series of proprietary calculations, are unveiled. The Kingsland Indices appear at jimkingsland.com to keep investors apprised of the latest changes in real estate, stocks, bonds, art, and, naturally, gold and silver bullion and collector coins.

There are two key indices, one that compiles collectibles as a group, and another that compiles coins and bullion as a group. As the art market has started to slump, there's a clear outperformance in coins and bullion.

■ **THE KINGSLAND ASSET INDEX**

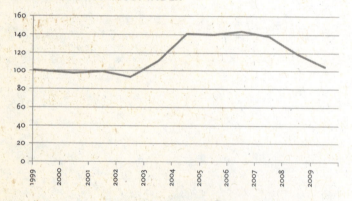

The Kingsland Asset Index. The base line for this index is 100 and the starting year for the index is 1999. The index has risen dramatically over the past 10 years due to a dramatic rise in a variety of bullion and coin-related products. Art has also been a contributing factor in the indices gain. However, real estate components have had a negative impact on the index over the last two years. The recent unraveling of the art market is also taking its toll.

The index measures:

1. Rare coins

2. Bullion

3. Collectible art

4. Farmland

5. Residential real estate

6. Corporate and government bonds

7. The dollar

■ **THE KINGSLAND GOLD AND SILVER ASSET INDEX**

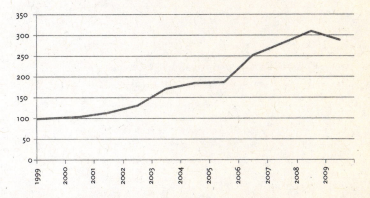

The Kingsland Gold and Silver Asset Index. This index also has a base line start at 100 and measures 100 coins. While gold has soared about threefold, the index has jumped by more than fourfold. The index also shows a steadier performance versus more volatile bullion precious metals and base metals prices. Here again is further confirmation that metals-related investments can indeed reward investor and speculator alike.

5
VALUE TRENDS IN COPPER

Just a few years ago people were literally dying to get their hands on copper. When it was almost triple the price it is today, copper suddenly started disappearing from construction sites, cell-phone towers, and even the New York City transit system. People were stealing it in hopes of turning it in to a scrap-metal yard and making a fast buck. Unfortunately, in some cases these expeditions turned out to be deadly: Hapless criminals fell from towers or were electrocuted in the process of stripping copper from live electrical equipment. To this day, there are isolated reports of copper thefts, as word has apparently been slow in getting to thieves that the copper bull market ended in 2008 and the metal is now only worth about $1.50 per pound versus the high-flying 2007 prices of more than four dollars per pound.

COPPER SUPERLATIVES

Dig deep enough and you'll find an organization that represents the interests of just about any industry. Copper is no exception. The Copper Development Association, a market development, engineering, and information services organization for the copper industry, was chartered to enhance and expand markets for copper and its alloys in North America. Its Web site, Copper.org, contains a treasure trove of information about copper: how much of it there is in the world, price trends, its history, who's using it—to cite just a few examples.

Copper.org also highlights the role copper is playing in the development in fuel-efficient hybrid car engines. A brighter future for all of us is on the way thanks to copper, it proclaims, namely because in cutting-edge hybrid engines two copper-wound electric motors are built into the drive train to enhance fuel efficiency.

For ten thousand years—long before the invention of the wheel, let alone hybrid engines—copper has been intertwined with human history. The U.S. Geological Survey calls copper "one of the most important materials in the development of civilization." It was the first mineral extracted from the earth by man, mined as early as 9,000 B.C., and used in the manufacture of some of man's earliest tools of industry. The discovery of bronze, an alloy formed when copper is melted with tin, heralded the start of the Bronze Age.

After one hundred centuries of use by humans, copper is anything but obsolete; in fact, it's more important than ever, and is ranked behind iron and aluminum as the world's third most consumed industrial metal. The price and available supplies of copper are closely monitored for signals on the health of the worldwide economy. More than 40 percent of copper demand in the United States comes from building construction, where copper is used in electrical wires and cables (the metal is an excellent electrical conductor), roofing, and pipes for heating, ventilating, and plumbing. Another 22 percent, or 1.6 billion pounds, of copper is consumed in the manufacturing of electronic and electrical products; 10 percent of copper is used to build transportation equipment; and another 9 percent is used for industrial machinery.

Not surprisingly, in the current recession stockpiles of copper have risen and demand has lessened as economic activity in all corners of the globe has downshifted drastically. As a result the price of copper has been weak.

■ COMEX HIGH-GRADE COPPER PER POUND

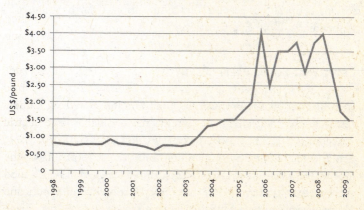

COMEX High-Grade Copper per Pound. *Data source: COMEX*

As important as U.S. demand is to the movement of copper, China has emerged as an even larger driving force in determining the metal's price. As exports of Chinese goods have slowed, the pace of the country's construction has slowed as well. In 2007, when China's economy was booming, copper consumption expanded by 36 percent, according to calculations by Reuters news service. Consumption was up only 7 percent in 2008.

COPPER IN U.S. COINAGE

When most people think about copper coins, they think cents, or pennies, but cents in the United States have long been less than 100 percent copper. Today's Lincoln penny is nearly all zinc (97.5 percent), with a thin copper coating—just enough to maintain that familiar copper cent look. Pure copper cents were minted only between 1793 and the mid-nineteenth century. These all-copper coins were called large cents, and were about the size of a modern-day quarter. After 1837, large cents struck by the U.S. Mint were made from varying compositions of copper with tin, zinc, and nickel (with the exception of the 1943 steel cent, produced during wartime when the United States was conserving copper). For precise coin compositions over the years, see Appendix A, Coin Specifications.

CENTS THAT COST A PRETTY PENNY

In January 2009, the Professional Coin Grading Service (PCGS) certified what it deemed the "world's most valuable large cent." The coin is a 1793 Strawberry Leaf graded at VG-10. This particular cent sold at a Stack's auction for a record $862,500. Only four of the coins are known to exist; three are graded by PCGS and one is held ungraded in the coin collection of the American Numismatic Society (ANS).

Only three months prior to the Stack's auction, a 1796 large cent briefly gained the distinction of the most valuable large cent. This post–Revolutionary War cent was auctioned in September 2008 by Ira and Larry Goldberg Auctioneers in Los Angeles for $690,000 on behalf of a private collector. The coin is graded MS-66 by PCGS, making it a very rare gem piece, free of corrosion and other problems that are associated with lower grades of coins from this era.

The Goldberg auction featured another ultra rarity: A "no pole" 1796 half-cent that fetched $345,000. Only thirty-two "no pole" uncirculated examples have been graded by PCGS.

A major rarity of this series of post–Revolutionary War coins is the 1793 Liberty Cap cent. It has been valued as high as four hundred thousand dollars in AU-55 BN (brown) condition—up 60 percent in the first half of 2009. It is a prime example of a coin whose value has risen consistently for decades, independently of the movements of underlying copper prices. An MS-63 example is priced at over $750,000. Even a low-grade example, with barely distinguishable features, will cost a collector more than seven thousand dollars.

The Liberty Cap held significant meaning in the post–Revolutionary War era. According to the coin-grading service Collectors Universe, "The Liberty Cap design features a bust of a young Miss Liberty, her hair flowing freely, with a staff and cap over her left shoulder. The cap represents freedom—hats such as this were given to slaves once they became free. The freedom cap was a popular symbol in America during the Revolutionary War, appearing on numerous buttons worn by patriots and soldiers. Miss Liberty represents the new American nation—her presence on the coin was mandated by government officials" (*www.collectorsuniverse.com*). Mintage of the coin was less than one million and only a few hundred have been certified. The moral to the story: Rarity is the collector's best friend when seeking insulation from swings in commodities prices and other economic uncertainties.

■ 1793 LIBERTY CAP 1-CENT PIECE

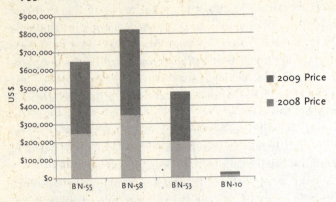

1793 Liberty Cap 1-Cent Piece.

The earliest U.S. cents of the 1790s were minted by the thousands and then by the tens of thousands. By the 1830s the Mint was running at full tilt and producing coins by the millions and then tens of millions each year thanks to innovations such as the steam press. With higher mintages but age on their side, common-date Flying Eagle cents (1856–1858) and Indian Head cents (1859–1909) remain affordable. Beautiful business-strike pennies for general circulation from the mid- to late nineteenth century in many cases trade for as little as five hundred dollars per coin in mint condition and have held their value well despite a recent downturn in the price of copper.

Bicentennial Lincoln Cent, 2009 reverse. *Photo courtesy of the U.S. Mint*

The same can be said for 95 percent–copper Lincoln "wheat cents" struck between 1909 and 1961 and during part of 1962: Value has managed to hold steady as time itself and rarity remain a coin collector's best friends. The most sought-after and valuable cents in the series are the famed Red (RD) 1909-S VDB (VDB being the initials of the coin's designer, Victor D. Brenner). The RD 1914-D, and RD 1922 "no D Strong Reverse" cents have also been performers that have maintained high value. The 1922 example is priced at one hundred thousand dollars in MS-64 condition with none graded higher by PCGS. Key-date Lincoln cents such as the 1909-S, 1914-D, and 1922 "Plain" varieties remain accessible to collectors with slightly deeper-than-average pockets. Finer examples are seeing some sag amid the recession.

▪ 1909 MS-65 VDB LINCOLN CENT RD

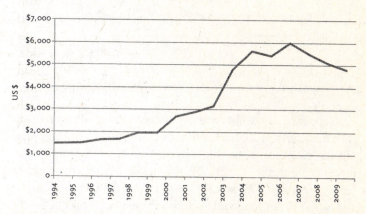

1909 MS-65 VDB Lincoln Cent RD. Prices on this chart reflect various auction results over the past 15 years. *Data source: Heritage Auction Galleries (HA.com)*

A mint-error coin can be worth a pretty penny. (For more on errors, see chapter 6, Value Trends in Base Metal Alloy Coins.) The collector value of the 1955 and 1972 doubled-die Lincoln cents far exceeds that of the metal they contain, though high-end examples have seen lower prices during the economic downturn.

The 1955 doubled-die-obverse cent has seen its value skyrocket relative to its non-error 1955 counterpart. The 1955 double die is also a standout example of a coin so sought after that even at the low end of the spectrum in F-12, the coin still commands a price of over one thousand dollars.

■ **1955 DOUBLED-DIE LINCOLN CENT RD**

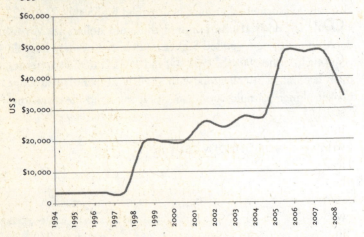

1955 Doubled-Die Lincoln Cent RD. *Data source: Heritage Auction Galleries (HA.com)*

Copper coins are not relegated to the world of the cent. Coins with a majority of copper are found across the coin spectrum and include two-cent pieces (95 percent copper), nickel three-cent pieces (75 percent copper), Shield nickels (75 percent copper), Jefferson nickels (75 percent copper), and Eisenhower dollars and Susan B. Anthony dollars (both 75 percent copper).

COPPER EXCHANGE-TRADED FUND AND BULLION

As of this writing, there are no Exchange-Traded Funds (ETFs) traded on U.S. stock exchanges that solely hold copper. The COPA ETF, designed to track the DJ-AIG Copper Sub-Index, is listed on the London Stock Exchange. (See chapter 7, Value Trends in Silver, for a more in-depth explanation of ETFs.)

Investors looking to buy copper bullion may do so through their trusted bullion dealer. A Google search of "copper bullion" yields a variety of dealers who can provide copper bullion in bar form.

COPPER FORECAST

Copper's performance was strong during the first six months of 2009, but in all financial market situations, uncertainty abounds. Through May 2009, copper put in upward performances for six straight months, surging by over 60 percent following a collapse in 2008. Copper advanced on the belief that economic growth will resume worldwide in 2010 with the United States and China leading the way. Whether the upswing is sustainable remains to be seen.

Rio Tinto Group, a mining company with stakes in the world's two largest copper mines, may be headed for a pullback in copper production. At a conference in London in 2009, Rio Tinto Copper chief executive Bret Clayton said that demand might not support the higher prices for copper. Clayton says it's possible that copper prices could decline in early 2010 because of what he calls an "uncertain" outlook. He is bullish, however, on copper's outlook over the next three to five years due to a lack of new discoveries and industry-wide supply constraints.

Patricia Mohr, economics and commodities markets specialist at Scotiabank Group, predicted at the World Mining Investment Congress in mid-2009 that copper prices at $1.95 per pound in 2010 were possible. She expects the metal to outperform other base metals.

6
VALUE TRENDS IN BASE METAL ALLOY COINS

Aside from the pure copper coinage of the late eighteenth and early nineteenth centuries, all coins are alloys, or mixed with more than one metal, which ensures the hardness of the coin and increases the time they take to wear down. American coinage for general circulation is no longer composed primarily of the precious metals gold and silver. Instead, they are made from a combination of base metals. Simply stated, base metals are relatively inexpensive metals that are readily available as ingredients in coins today. Copper, nickel, zinc, and manganese are examples of base metals used in modern coinage.

Base metal alloy coins are yet another example of the degraded quality of our money. While the coins of today look as attractive as American coins have for the past two centuries, they are fiat money, whose value is dictated by what society deems the money is worth, not by the actual melt value of the coin. As an example, a Morgan dollar that circulated in the nineteenth century was composed of 90 percent silver and 10 percent of the base metal copper, and today has a melt value of about eleven dollars; but a modern day Presidential dollar is made up of 6 percent zinc, 3.5 percent manganese, 2 percent nickel, and 88.5 percent copper, and has a melt value of about four cents.

Modern Lincoln cents (since 1982) are 97.5 percent zinc, with a copper coating to maintain the copper look of the penny, and presently has a melt value of less than a half-cent. The Jefferson nickel has a composition of 75 percent copper and 25 percent nickel (as it did when it was first introduced in 1938) and is worth around three cents. Washington quarters, Roosevelt dimes, and Kennedy half-dollars of today are made of a combination of copper and nickel known as cupronickel, which gives the coins their silver look, but little in the way of actual value. The Sacagawea and Presidential dollars get their golden appearance from a combination of metals: 88.5 percent copper, 6 percent zinc, 3.5 percent manganese, and 2 percent nickel. Even the 1943 steel Lincoln cent had a tiny dollop of zinc coating.

This chapter examines modern alloy coins (since the mid-1960s). Though these present-day alloy coins contain cheaper base metals as opposed to precious metals like gold, silver, or platinum, they have shown much larger swings in value than older gold, silver, and copper coins, due to the volatility of their base metal components over the last few years and due to the fact that much of what constitutes the worth of older, precious-metal coins is their age and rarity.

ZINC

The London Metals Exchange describes zinc, one of the most common modern alloy coin components, in this manner: "Zinc is commonly mined as a co-product with standard lead and both metals have growing core markets for their consumption. For zinc, the main market is galvanising, which accounts for almost half its modern-day demand. Zinc's electropositive nature enables metals to be readily galvanised, which gives added protection against corrosion to building structures, vehicles, machinery and household equipment."

NICKEL

Nickel was first isolated as its own metal ("primary nickel") in 1751. According to the London Metals Exchange, "prior to this, it was found in copper mines and thought to be an unsmeltable copper ore. Primary nickel can resist corrosion and maintains its physical and mechanical properties even when placed under extreme temperatures. When these properties were recognised, the development of primary nickel began. It was found that by combining primary nickel with steel, even in small quantities, the durability and strength of the steel increased significantly as did its resistance to corrosion. This partnership has remained and the production of stainless steel is now the single largest consumer of primary nickel today. This highly useful metal is also used in the production of many different metal alloys for specialised use."

MANGANESE

The U.S. Geologic Survey's database describes manganese as being "essential to iron and steel production by virtue of its sulfur-fixing, deoxidizing, and alloying properties." It goes on to say that "steelmaking, including its ironmaking component, has accounted for most manganese demand, presently in the range of 85 percent to 90 percent of the total demand. Among a variety of other uses, manganese is a key component of low cost."

In addition to being a component of the Sacagawea and Presidential dollars, manganese was used in wartime nickels produced from 1942 to 1945.

THE IMPLICATIONS OF VOLATILITY IN BASE METALS

When zinc surged to as high as two dollars per pound in 2007, the U.S. Mint suddenly had a $100-million problem on its hands. It was losing that amount of money minting coins, because the base metal cost had soared.

More than forty years earlier the Mint thought it had the problem of high commodities costs licked when it eliminated silver from U.S. coinage through the Coinage Act of 1965. And then in 1982 the Mint changed the penny from a composition of 90 percent more expensive copper, to 97.5 percent cheaper zinc with just 2.5 percent copper. But by 2006, the inflation in base metals (some call it "coin-flation") returned with a vengeance as a bubble developed in a variety of commodities from aluminum to zinc. Under normal conditions, the mostly zinc-clad penny should have a melt value of a fraction of a cent and the silver-less Roosevelt dime of today should have a melt value of a few cents. Similarly, Jefferson nickels normally have a melt value of three cents, but not so during that brief stretch of time in 2006 and 2007 when the Mint was losing millions.

The Mint was becoming a laughingstock. Reports in the media were rhetorically asking, "Who else but the government would pay almost two cents for a penny?" Edmund Moy, director of the Mint, told House lawmakers at the time, "With each new penny and nickel we issue, we also increase the national debt by almost as much as the coin is worth, and these losses are rapidly mounting."

Fortunately for the Mint, commodities slumped by late 2008 and the melt values of pennies and nickels that are minted today returned to being a fraction of their face values. Pre-1982, mostly-copper pennies are holding on to a melt value of about one and a half cents.

THE MINT SAYS NO MELTING

The temporary rise in the value of the coins' component metals prompted some people to think about nearly doubling their money by melting cents and nickels. That led the U.S. Mint to declare the melting of these coins illegal. The Mint feared that industrious individuals with blow torches in hand would create a shortage of cents and nickels by melting them. Mint Director Moy approved an interim rule on December 12, 2006. He said, "the new rule safeguards the integrity of U.S. coinage and protects taxpayers from bearing the costs to replace coins withdrawn from circulation. The rising commodity prices of copper, nickel, and zinc have increased the value of the metal in both pennies and nickels so that the content of these coins now exceeds their face value. There is concern that speculators could remove pennies and nickels from circulation and sell them as scrap for profit."

Moy at the time said penalties would be harsh for coin melting profiteers, "The new regulation authorizes a fine of not more than ten thousand dollars, or imprisonment of not more than five years, or both, against a person who knowingly violates the regulation. In addition, by law, any coins exported, melted, or treated in violation of the regulation shall be forfeited to the United States Government."

MINTING COINS IS A HUGE TASK

While things have settled down where coin melting is concerned, the Mint finds itself operating in an environment where it can't keep up with demand for special products like certain gold and platinum coins.

However, the Mint has not come up short in the production of coinage for everyday use. Last year, production of all circulating coins (penny, nickel, dime, quarter, half dollar, and dollar) totaled over 10 billion pieces.

The Mint accomplishes this gargantuan task at its facilities in Philadelphia, Pennsylvania, and Denver, Colorado. The Mint's San Francisco branch is the manufacturer of regular proof and silver proof coin sets. The Mint facility at West Point, New York manufactures the entire family of American Eagle proof and uncirculated coins in gold, silver, and platinum.

THE 50 STATE QUARTERS PROGRAM

A huge influx of new coin collectors in recent years has been due to the attention-grabbing performance of precious metals, and in larger measure to far-ranging programs rolled out by the U.S. Mint. The Sacagawea Dollar and Presidential Dollar programs and most popularly the 50 State Quarters Program, which started in 1999, have attracted new collectors in droves. Once word got out about valuable error coins that escaped from the Mint, a frenzied pace of collecting set in.

The 50 State Quarters Program was the first of its kind by the U.S. Mint. Beginning in 1999 the Mint stopped production of the Washington Quarter, instead issuing legal-tender quarters commemorating each of the fifty states. Five state designs were released per year over a period of ten years, issued in the order in which the states were admitted to the Union. The program officially ended in 2008, but the Mint added six more designs for 2009 to recognize the nation's capital and five territories.

To say the program was a raving success is an understatement. The federal government estimates that it has earned nearly $6 billion in seigniorage revenue from the decade-long State Quarters Program because of the vast numbers of quarters taken out of circulation by collectors and resulting increased production by the Mint. The program was lucrative for some investors as well. Those who bought rolls, bags, and boxes of quarters from banks and discovered near-perfect to perfect-70 statehood coins instantly hit the jackpot, now in possession of quarters worth thousands of dollars, in pristine condition. Error state quarters (see below) are also worth their weight in gold.

COSTLY AND VALUABLE ERRORS

Even though coins struck today are composed of base metals rather than more valuable precious metals, certain speculative coins are emerging. These are mostly due to errors that occur at the Mint. In most walks of life errors are negative occurrences. In numismatics, errors can be wealth-creating opportunities. And that's a good thing, considering that the billions of coins spewed from our Mints each year are worth just their face value once spent and are likely, in circulated form, to remain at face value for many decades to come. Spotting an error in your pocket change can rescue a valuable coin from obscurity.

Errors that can mean big money for collectors are broadstrikes, double strikes, and off-center die cuts. A broadstrike is a coin that made its way into a coin press without a retaining collar inside the part of the machine that strikes the coin. It results in a coin that is spread out—thinner and larger than normal pieces. Double-struck coins are those struck more than once while being made. Off-center coins, as their name implies, are coins struck from a misaligned die or planchet, resulting in a misplaced image.

STATE QUARTER ERRORS

A double-struck State Quarter can command a price of as much as one thousand dollars, according to U.S. error coins Web site CoinSite (*www.coinsite.com*). Off-center and broadstruck State Quarters can be worth between one hundred dollars and $150 apiece and sometimes more, depending upon the degree of damage the coin has suffered. The 2004-D Wisconsin Extra Leaf High quarter (which has a die error that resembles an extra leaf on an ear of corn) in the grade of MS-67 commands the highest value among regular-strike state quarters at fifteen thousand dollars, according to the Professional Coin Grading Service (PCGS).

PRESIDENTIAL ONE DOLLAR ERRORS

Some of the most valuable errors of recent date come from the new Presidential dollars in which inscriptions IN GOD WE TRUST, E PLURIBUS UNUM, and/or the mint mark and year were omitted. An error Washington one dollar piece with a grade of MS-67 can command bids of over two thousand dollars, and that's with more than one hundred thousand of the uncirculated error coins known to be in existence. A rarer satin finish Adams one dollar coin, with only a little more than one hundred coins known to exist, can fetch well over ten thousand dollars.

AN OLD RULE RINGS TRUE: DON'T SEND MONEY THROUGH THE MAIL

The coin hobby is running hot and 150 million strong. Hobby activity is so robust that dealers have noted increased thefts of coins being sent through the U.S. Postal Service. The Postmaster General's Office wouldn't comment on that, but a number of dealers maintain that packages of coins have mysteriously vanished en route from Point A to Point B. To ensure that your coins arrive safely through the mail, be sure that they are shipped via higher security Registered Mail.

THE FORECAST FOR BASE METALS

The performance of base metals is tied to worldwide industrial demand, which is controlled by the state of the world economy. While economic forecasters see a return to economic growth in 2010, the growth may be tepid at best, meaning somewhat hampered upward price movements for base metals. Should this scenario play out, the melt values of pennies, nickels, and dimes should remain fairly stable in 2010, unless a sudden pickup in inflation causes commodities, including base metals, to soar. The main indicator of price movement for base-metal-clad coins will likely be the discovery of error coins.

THE OUTLOOK FOR ZINC

Will the penny return to a melt value of 1.7 cents because of a renewed surge in the price of zinc? That's an unlikely scenario unless a new boom in commodities or general hyperinflation comes to pass. For now, the consensus is comfortable with a slowdown in the world economy that will stunt demand in base metals and keep their prices in check. At British banking giant Barclays Capital, metals analysts see a stable zinc price, though they expect zinc mining output will decline. "All in all, we estimate that [excluding China], around 550,000 metric tons of production capacity, equivalent to almost 5 percent of global output, has been closed," said a Barclays report. Lower mining output will at least maintain a floor under zinc.

THE OUTLOOK FOR NICKEL

The situation for nickel is similar to many mining stories of recent months: Production is being curtailed due to slower demand in the wake of the financial crisis. The International Nickel Study Group (INSG) based in Lisbon, Portugal, which tracks all things nickel through representatives of both the nickel industry and producing countries, says that until stainless steel demand picks up, it's not likely that nickel demand will pick up. The INSG doesn't anticipate stronger stainless steel production until economic growth accelerates in early 2010.

7
VALUE TRENDS IN SILVER

Silver is indeed precious. As the Silver Institute puts it, "Although silver is relatively scarce, it is the most plentiful and least expensive of the precious metals. Besides signifying status and wealth, silver has been one of the most romantic and sought after of all the precious metals. From the beginning of time people have been enthralled by its beauty and drawn to remote areas of the world in search of this white, reflective metal."

Also known as "white gold," silver has been a medium of financial exchange for more than two thousand years—found in the first known coinage of the eastern Mediterranean dating to about 500 B.C. Silver was the primary original component of the once valuable Roman denarius (used from the second century B.C. through the second century A.D.), which ultimately died when it was debased—mixed with other metals to the point of containing virtually no silver. To this day, silver persists in coinage form, in bullion and commemorative issues struck by the U.S. Mint, but it is gone, since 1965, from business-strike U.S. coins. Only Mexico currently uses limited amounts of silver in the coins it produces for circulation.

THE "CRIME OF 1873"

The founders of the United States established silver and gold as mediums of exchange in the nation's first coinage act in 1792 (see Appendix B), creating a bimetallic monetary standard. The act set the value of gold to silver at a 15:1 ratio. But change came to the ratio in the latter part of the nineteenth century. As silver became devalued by more discoveries and a larger supply, nations around the world switched to a pure gold standard and the gold-to-silver ratio ultimately increased to 40:1. In 1873 the United States left the bimetallic standard in the Coinage Act of 1873 for gold, causing silver advocates to brand the move the "Crime of 1873."

The debate over silver's role in the U.S. monetary system would fiercely rage on for decades to come and would have an especially strong impact on the presidential election of 1896. The tumultuous race to the White House would give rise to the terms "gold bugs" (fans of gold) and "silver bugs" (those who favor silver).

America was a nation on the rise and moving to the center of the global stage in 1896. As our economy was maturing and expanding in the late nineteenth century, issues involving money and an ever-growing demand for investment capital were becoming more complex and in some cases divisive.

Gold and silver were on the minds of Americans, from the poorest of the poor to the working classes to the mightiest of business titans in 1896. A stock market collapse in 1893, known as the Panic of 1893, followed on the heels of a worldwide depression that started two decades earlier in 1873 (later named the Long Depression) and came about in part due to the shift to the gold standard that turned out to have deflationary economic consequences when gold supplies diminished. Thus the populace was gripped in a national debate over whether our money should be backed by gold, otherwise known as the gold standard or "sound money," or whether more silver coinage should be added back into circulation—a position known as "free silver coinage."

The greater use of silver would have increased total money in circulation: a good thing for a weak economy, claimed the silver proponents. The opponents within the gold camp maintained that more silver coinage would dilute the money supply and increase inflation, something they ominously labeled the "silver menace."

In 1896, it was an all-out political battle between William McKinley, the Republican presidential candidate who favored the gold standard, versus William Jennings Bryan, the Democrat who supported silver coinage.

McKinley proclaimed in his nomination acceptance letter:

> We have had few questions in the lifetime of the Republic more serious than the one which is presented. We must not be misled by phrases, nor deluded by false theories. Free silver would not mean that silver dollars were to be freely had without cost or labor. It would mean the free use of the mints of the United States for the few who are owners of silver bullion, but would make silver coin no

freer to the many who are engaged in other enterprises.... Until international agreement is had it is the plain duty of the United States to maintain the gold standard. It is the recognized and sole standard of the great commercial nations of the world, with which we trade more largely than any other....[1]

Bryan became famous for his fiery speech at the Democratic National Convention in Chicago, where he wryly concluded:

If they dare to come out in the open field and defend the gold standard as a good thing, we shall fight them to the uttermost, having behind us the producing masses of the nation and the world. Having behind us the commercial interests and the laboring interests and all the toiling masses, we shall answer their demands for a gold standard by saying to them, you shall not press down upon the brow of labor this crown of thorns. You shall not crucify mankind upon a cross of gold![2]

And so the battle lines were drawn. The election of 1896 was a bitter gold-versus-silver fight for the White House and, in economic terms, was perhaps the nation's most important election until the 2008 contest. The sound-money advocates, or gold bugs, were ultimately victorious, with McKinley taking the election. The defeat of Bryan is still debated and studied by scholars today. Many say Bryan had no chance because of opposition from financial institutions and power brokers of the time. Others point to a too-loud, shrill, and excessively populist campaign by Bryan.

The many virtuous arguments in support of one standard or another are long gone, since today our currency is backed by nothing—neither gold nor silver. In stark contrast to the "bailout era" we find ourselves in now, the power brokers of 1896 found

---

[1] William Jennings Bryan, *The First Battle* (Chicago: W. B. Conkey Company, 1896), ch. xxvii, p. 392.

[2] *Official Proceedings of the Democratic National Convention Held in Chicago, Ill., July 7th, 8th, 9th, 10th, and 11th, 1896* (Logansport, IN: Wilson, Humphries & Co., 1896), 226–234.

the quick fix that silver might have brought to the money supply unpalatable. McKinley's preaching of "honor" on the world stage and the need to adhere to sound money struck a chord among many of that era but is foreign in our present age.

THE HUNTS AND BUFFETT

The more ardent of silver's advocates today argue that if the financial world as we know it comes to an end—in a post-paper-money world—silver will jump (from current levels of fourteen dollars an ounce) to fifty to one hundred dollars an ounce or more and be easier to use in business transactions than the more expensive gold. (Again, this is an extreme-viewpoint theory.)

But you don't need to be stocking the cupboards with cans of tuna fish, ready-to-eat meals, and ammunition to be a fan of silver. Billionaire businessmen have at times taken an extreme liking to what the Silver Institute characterizes as the "indispensable metal."

For "silver bugs" (those bullish on silver) a price above the 1980 record of forty-nine dollars remains the holy grail and a minimum price target. In January 1980, silver came within striking distance of fifty dollars, but collapsed after an effort by Nelson Bunker Hunt and his brother Herbert to corner the silver market eventually unraveled. The Hunt brothers amassed a 100-million-ounce holding of silver, earning more than a billion dollars in speculative activity in the futures market tied to their silver hoard before commodities exchange officials changed cash requirements, forcing the brothers to sell at a loss.

Not to be outdone, billionaire investor Warren Buffett tried to create his own silver streak and in 2001 announced that his Berkshire Hathaway holding company had accumulated 129 million ounces. Silver prices shot up by two dollars an ounce on the basis of the disclosure. But Buffett's romance with silver would prove to be just a brief fling, uncharacteristic for a man known for buying and holding assets for decades. A Berkshire Hathaway annual report in the spring of 2006 disclosed that Buffett had sold the family silver—all of it.

Since then, silver has more than doubled in price to present-day levels above fourteen dollars an ounce. "I bought it very early, I sold it very early. Other than that, it was perfect," Buffett chuckled at the time. Some have speculated that Buffett actually lost his silver hoard in the futures market, but Buffett has been mum.

Although silver's slide from a 2008 high above twenty dollars to ten dollars by late 2008 was as spectacular as any implosion in commodities during that tumultuous year—a decline of nearly 50 percent—the bottom line for silver is that even with 2008's monumental decline it has been a strong performer, by and large, over the last ten years. Rising from a nadir in the four dollar range, silver is worth more than triple what it was a decade ago.

THE SILVER-TO-GOLD RATIO

Gold and silver bulls are excited over something called the silver-to-gold ratio—which, in simplest terms, measures the amount of silver needed to buy an ounce of gold. Watchers of this index say the lower the ratio goes, or the less silver it takes to buy gold, the more bullish the outlook for both silver and gold. The general trend since silver's 2008 low of about ten dollars an ounce is that the ratio has narrowed. It's simply one indicator that shows demand and interest in silver is strong, which has had positive implications for gold. The ratio has narrowed from 80:1 in 2008 to a more recent 60:1.

The amount of silver it takes to buy an ounce of gold has been contracting recently. That's a bullish trend, according to some silver and gold analysts, and keeps specimens like silver Trade dollars and Morgan dollars (shown here) in healthy demand. *Image courtesy of the Numismatic Guaranty Corporation*

SUPPLY AND DEMAND—
SILVER MARKET CONDITIONS

Silver supply and demand is driven by a variety of factors. On the demand side, we are seeing an increased need for silver in industrial applications—primarily in electrical and electronic sectors (silver is an excellent conductor of electricity)—and in forging coins and medals. On the other hand, the use of silver in photography has fallen steadily over the last ten years due to an increase in digital photography, as has its use in jewelry and silverware.

The Silver Supply Institute, an industry watchdog, reported a 1 percent rise in total global silver fabrication demand, to 843.7 million ounces, in 2007. Industrial application demand jumped by more than 7 percent with the United States, China, and India during 2007, accounting for 70 percent of worldwide use of silver in industrial application.

On the supply side, mine production and the supply of silver scrap have risen during the last ten years, according to the Silver Supply Institute. The only supply-side category to experience a decline over the last decade is global government sales of silver. The Silver Supply Institute reported an overall 4 percent rise in 2007 silver production paced by healthy supply coming from Peru, Mexico, China, and Chile. Of the top five producers of silver in the world, Peru leads, supplying 112 million ounces per year and contributing mightily to overall world silver production of 670 million ounces, followed by Mexico, China, Chile, and Australia. The United States ranks as the eighth largest silver producer.

Though production levels have increased, net supply has actually declined due to a reduction in government sales of silver and an unwinding of hedges by silver producers who had capped prices. Aboveground silver inventories declined by 8 percent in 2007 to 173 million ounces. Sales of silver by China and India were practically nonexistent in 2007, contributing to a near 50 percent reduction in total government sales.

The combination of increased industrial demand and a decline in government sales has corresponded with a rise in the price of the metal from a turn-of-the-twenty-first-century trough of just over four dollars an ounce to present double-digit levels of fourteen dollars.

WAYS TO INVEST

Beyond buying actual physical silver bullion in bar, round, or coin form, investors can also buy exchange-traded funds or derivatives in the futures and options markets, and/or rare collector coins. What you decide to do is partly up to your gut and what feels best for you, but there are some definite pros and cons to each type of investment.

SILVER BULLION

Not surprisingly, the combination of economic factors that have led to a rise in demand for metals has led to a sharp increase in purchases of silver American Eagle bullion coins from the U.S. Mint (see chart below).

▪ U.S. MINT SILVER BULLION SALES

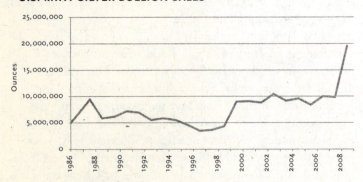

U.S. Mint Silver Bullion Sales. *Data source: U.S. Mint*

Strong demand for silver is also evident on online auction services like eBay, where it is not uncommon to see silver rounds and bars trading for up to three dollars per ounce above spot market prices. Not only are the premiums large, but the bidding can be fierce with dozens of offers being made up to the final seconds of various auctions. Auctions on eBay have featured a full spectrum of silver products, from silver American Eagles, to one-ounce silver rounds, to one hundred–ounce Engelhard bars of silver—all quickly scooped up by bidders who may be looking for a hedge against potential future fiscal disaster.

NON-BULLION SILVER COINS

The strength of silver's price has led to a generally strong performance in the value of silver coinage. Charts of silver coins consistently show prices taking off once the nation abandoned all vestiges of the gold standard in the early 1970s. From that point onward, assets related to gold and silver began to shoot up as the dollar saw its buying power diminish.

While silver coins of the greatest rarity and value continued to cost a pretty penny for even the richest of the rich, big-ticket silver coins more accessible to a broader population of collectors have declined in value, or have stopped increasing in value. Some contrasting examples follow.

A 1794 Draped Bust silver dollar is a standout. Where the earliest U.S. coinage is concerned, prices and trends have operated above and independently from the hustle and bustle of the silver market.

▪ 1794 DRAPED BUST SILVER DOLLAR XF-40

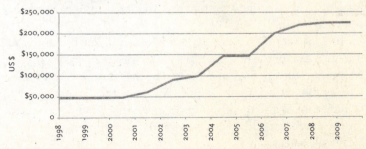

1794 Draped Bust Silver Dollar XF-40. *Data source: Heritage Auction Galleries (HA.com)*

In contrast to coins that are nearly two hundred years old, the relatively recent 1952 Franklin half-dollar (in MS-60 condition) shows volatility due to underlying conditions in the silver market.

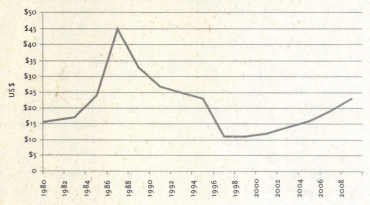

1952 Franklin Half-Dollar MS-60. *Data source: Heritage Auction Galleries (HA.com)*

Age is no indicator of premium value when it comes to collector coins. For example, the beautiful but common 1887 Morgan silver dollar certified in the high grade of MS-65 by PCGS sells for less than two hundred dollars. About 20 million examples were produced.

In contrast, in October 2008 a Morgan dollar broke the $1 million mark for the first time. The grand specimen was an 1893-S Morgan, graded MS-67 and verified by the Certified Acceptance Corporation (CAC) coin-verification authority. Laura Sperber of rare-coin firm Legend Numismatics, who acted as the proxy for the purchaser of the coin, was quoted as saying that her client "really likes neat coins."

■ MORGAN SILVER DOLLAR MS-65

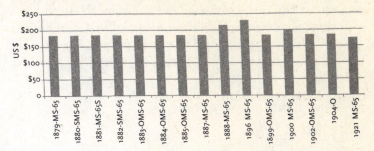

Common Date Morgan Silver Dollar Prices in MS-65. *Data source: Heritage Auction Galleries (HA.com)*

The super-rare 1804 Draped Bust silver dollar, which was struck more than thirty years after the date it bears, is the ultimate coin to buy, hold, and pass down. It has commanded auction prices of more than $1 million. The so-called Dexter and Adams-Carter specimens (named after owners of the coin) passed through many hands and auctions—rising from a paltry value of two hundred dollars in the 1800s to seven-figure values today. Only fifteen of the coins are known to exist.

■ 1804 "DEXTER" SILVER DOLLAR PR-64

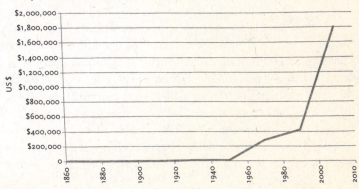

1804 "Dexter" Silver Dollar PR-64. *Data source: Numismatic Guaranty Corporation (NGC)*

What about the average coin? The Professional Coin Grading Service (PCGS) has its own index of three thousand coins, which as of this writing is down a bit more than 4 percent from its 2008 peak. But in the grand scheme of things, a 4 percent decline is a mere blip on a chart that shows stupendous gains over nearly forty years.

▪ PCGS 3000 INDEX (1970 TO DATE)

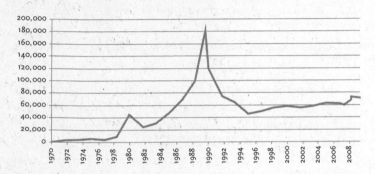

PCGS 3000 Index (1970 to Date). *Data source: Professional Coin Grading Service (PCGS.com)*

Junk Silver

One man's junk is another man's treasure. This seems especially true with certain pre-1965 U.S. coins. The end of 1964 witnessed the demise of silver dimes and quarters. Kennedy half-dollars lived on in 40-percent-silver form from 1965 to 1970, and 40-percent-silver Eisenhower dollars were minted from 1971 to 1976. As the government switched to cheaper alloys in the dimes, quarters, and half-dollars, the more valuable silver currency that remained in circulation quickly disappeared. It was hoarded—an inevitable result when more valuable coinage is replaced with a less-expensive version.

The hoarded silver pocket change is reappearing and has become popular with some investors and collectors, who buy large quantities—generally thousand-dollar bags—in hopes that silver will rise even further and make the intrinsic value of the old, shabby change even greater.

Melt values are already up hundreds of percent from face value, and buyers of "junk silver" take comfort from the fact that there's a floor beneath the silver coins—their face value. Bags of junk silver can still be obtained from various dealers for modest premiums over melt value.

If you're a fan of silver and you expect that it will continue to rise, so-called junk silver is probably one of the easiest ways to acquire silver. But finding space to store heavy bags of silver change can be a challenge.

Gems in Pocket Change and Elsewhere

A phenomenon that continues to spur interest in coins is finding gems in everyday pocket change and through other avenues of procurement. While the odds are low that the average person will stumble upon a coin jingling in his pocket worth thousands—or even tens of thousands—of dollars, such windfall events have occurred.

In 2009, the American Numismatic Association Certification Service (ANACS) coin-grading service received a 1792 silver-center cent for authentication and certification from an anonymous collector. Only fourteen examples of this coin are known to exist today. According to ANACS, "The owner ... purchased the coin at a local police auction for four hundred dollars, the amount he insured it for when he sent it to ANACS. It is estimated today to be worth at least three hundred thousand dollars." (For a discussion of buying non-bullion error coins, see chapter 6, Value Trends in Base Metal Alloy Coins.)

EXCHANGE TRADED FUNDS—BUYER BEWARE?

Exchange Traded Funds (ETFs) for precious metals are fairly new to the market. The Barclays iShares silver ETF made its sterling debut in 2006 and was an instant success. It's the only ETF of its kind available to investors in the United States seeking to capture price moves in silver. The silver ETF trades under the ticker symbol of SLV on the New York Stock Exchange.

One of the most positive contributions of the Exchange Traded Funds is that they create demand for the metals they are associated with. Metals ETFs are a way to capitalize on the growing popularity of metals without having to hold and store the physical metals. But there are distinct differences between—and some serious disadvantages of—holding an ETF share versus holding the physical metal. What you are buying with an ETF is convenience, not a stake in a physical metal that can be delivered upon demand. When you buy shares of a metal in an Exchange Traded Fund (ETF) you are *not* buying ownership in the actual underlying metal that's held by the ETF—you are buying into a fund. This means that you will never be able to withdraw gold, silver, or platinum; you can only sell your shares for dollars.

As with all investments, it's important to read the prospectus carefully and consult with a registered investment advisor. It is especially important to consider the disclaimer language at the start of all prospectuses. The following is from the prospectus of iShares Silver Trust.

> Investing involves risk, including possible loss of principal. Because shares of the iShares Silver Trust are expected to reflect the price of the silver held by the iShares Silver Trust, the market price of the shares will be as unpredictable as the price of silver has historically been. Additionally, shares of the Silver Trust are bought and sold at market price (not NAV [net asset value]). Brokerage commissions will reduce returns.

It's no great revelation that silver is volatile, which affects both the physical metals investor and the silver ETF investor. The iShares prospectus bluntly warns investors of the uncertainty of the silver market and the unpredictability of returns on silver ETF investments, saying, "The price of silver has fluctuated widely over the past several years. If silver markets continue to be characterized by the wide fluctuations that they have shown in the past several years, the price of the iShares will change widely and in an unpredictable manner. This exposes your investment in iShares to potential losses if you need to sell your iShares at a time when the price of silver is lower than it was when you made your investment in iShares. Even if you are able to hold iShares for the mid- or long-term you may never realize a profit, because silver markets have historically experienced extended periods of flat or declining prices."

The iShares prospectus itself calls an investment in the iShares Silver ETF "an investment *similar to* an investment in silver" (emphasis added)—that's "similar" but not the same as investing in physical silver. The ETF is but a paper instrument that tracks the price of silver and may decline in value over time due to expenses (such as trust, sponsor, and bookkeeping fees and administrative and advertising costs), even if the value of the physical metal holds steady. How to make up for those expenses? By selling off silver in the fund. Unless the price of silver increases over time, in order to maintain the value of the fund, silver is sold to meet expenses. Another disadvantage is the potential for any number of unexpected liabilities that aren't specified in the prospectus.

It's also important to know where the fund's physical silver is stored and who controls it. According to the iShares Web site, its Silver Trust holds over 270 million ounces of silver. This is more than eight thousand tons of silver that, according to the iShares prospectus, is not held in a specific location since the fund's custodian has the right to designate other custodians to hold silver for the trust. There is no camera trained on the silver, there is simply the word of iShares that somewhere there is more than eight thousand tons of silver held for the benefit of the ETF. So ultimately, that the assets to back your investment actually exist is a matter of faith.

And keeping track of the institutions involved in managing the funds is no easy feat. While Barclays is the iShares Trust sponsor, the Bank of New York acts as trustee in charge of the daily administration of the ETF, and J.P. Morgan is the custodian responsible for safekeeping the silver owned by the trust. Critics of ETFs have suggested that, since the silver isn't held in a single location, there's room for the sponsors and custodians to fudge figures on exact holdings. Such accusations are harsh, but perhaps not ludicrous given the problems financial institutions have created for themselves recently.

No two investors are alike. While a longer-term holding in physical metals would seem more attractive than a paper metal asset with various expenses to some, others may be drawn to the relative convenience and speculative nature of ETFs.

STORING YOUR METALS

The issue of buying physical silver, or any other metal, versus paper-form ETF shares or futures inevitably leads to the issue of storage. Taken on the whole, the fact that the silver ETF can end up selling its physical silver to meet expenses is a negative for holders of the ETF shares. Why not acquire silver and store it for little or no cost?

First and foremost is the issue of whom you can trust to hold physical metals. As one investor found out, he was unable to trust Wall Street giant Morgan Stanley. He sued the mega-firm and forced Morgan Stanley to settle in 2008. The case involved an investor who thought Morgan Stanley was buying and storing silver for him.

The plaintiff in the case, Selwyn Silberblatt, forced Morgan Stanley to pay $4.4 million to settle a class-action lawsuit with brokerage clients who bought precious metals and paid storage fees. According to the suit, Morgan Stanley had told clients it would buy and store silver for them, but Silberblatt discovered that in fact no silver had been stored. Morgan Stanley settled the case, allegedly to avoid costly litigation.

The Silberblatt case is another instance of buyer beware. Just because a venerable name is providing a service doesn't mean it can automatically be trusted. If choosing a depository, the investor should insist that his or her metals are not comingled with the holdings of other investors to ensure withdrawal in a timely manner. Experts say that individuals looking to store metals and coinage at home should invest in a heavy-duty safe that can be bolted to the floor, installed by a trusted security company. Top-notch security companies guarantee confidentiality, but it's up to the investor to keep the fact that a home safe exists a secret. More and more popular (and not a bad idea) are safes that are not only burglar-proof and fireproof but also explosion-proof and able to withstand temperatures of up to three hundred degrees Fahrenheit.

SILVER FORECASTS

In the first half of 2009, the price of silver has steadily increased, moving in tandem with a general rebound in commodities like gold and oil. (Commodities denominated in dollars tend to rise when the dollar falls as it simply takes more of the weaker dollars to buy the same commodities.) As usual, forecasts for future price movement in silver and all commodities vary greatly since they are guesses—perhaps not even educated guesses, but merely akin to throwing a dart at a board and seeing where it sticks.

Not everyone is a fan of silver; just ask analysts Barry Cooper, Brian Quast, and Cosmos Chiu at the Canadian Imperial Bank of Commerce, better known as CIBC. They not only maintain an eleven-dollar-an-ounce forecast (a drop in price) for silver in 2010, but flatly declare that "holding gold is better than holding silver." The analysts see silver's fall from more than twenty dollars an ounce in 2008 as a solid indication that silver is moving more in line with industrial metals than with gold.

But, as discussed earlier in the chapter, the narrowing silver-to-gold ratio has silver proponents feeling bullish. James Turk, the editor of the *Freemarket Gold and Money Report*, an investment newsletter analyzing the precious metals, commodities, and financial markets, predicts that the ratio will continue to fall, and says that this will result in substantially higher price levels for silver.

"Last year, the gold-to-silver ratio repeatedly tested overhead resistance in the low 80s," Turk said, adding, "from its highest peak, the ratio has dropped 17.6 percent, which is by any measure a very healthy gain achieved in less than four months." That, Turk was quoted as saying in a recent *MarketWatch* article[3], could send silver to as high as forty-five dollars an ounce if the ratio falls to levels seen in 1980—the last time silver soared to stratospheric highs.

Given the fiscal ills of the nation, which have brought to the surface questions about the credit quality of the United States and cast doubt on whether the United States is entitled to a Aaa rating, precious metals are particularly attractive for their intrinsic store of value. Thus the outlook is bullish for all precious metals, including silver. The evidence has already been seen in the price performance of silver, up more than 80 percent from 2008 lows and destined to climb even more if the dollar falls farther and commodities move higher. In this author's estimation there is likely a better than 70 percent chance that silver will retest its 2008 highs in the twenty dollar an ounce range should the dollar continue to fall.

---

[3] Peter Brimelow, "Something New Stirring in Precious-Metals Pond," MarketWatch (Feb. 8, 2009), http://www.marketwatch.com/story/something-new-stirring-precious-metals-pond.

8
VALUE TRENDS IN GOLD

In the annals of modern finance, gold—no longer standard in world currencies—has been the focal point for investors looking to hedge against the worst-case economic scenarios, namely the collapse of the dollar, the collapse of the economy, or both. (And indeed, if the dollar is toppled in favor of an international currency, as China has recently called for, gold investors may have the last laugh.) Even those who don't foresee an end to the economy as we know it tend to consider gold a hedge against inflation, pointing to its unwavering purchasing power: Whether four hundred years ago or today, an ounce of the yellow metal should buy a man a fine suit of clothes. And now, as the Fed prints dollars with reckless abandon to save the economy from a deflationary depression, many investors are betting the value of the dollar will continue to fall.

There's a simple rule at work: Gold is ruled by the dollar. Jim Sinclair, a precious metals specialist, commodities and foreign currency trader, and founder of Jim Sinclair's MineSet (*www.jsmineset.com*), is widely credited with spreading the word on that rule. Translated, the rule means that when the dollar rises gold shall fall and when the dollar falls gold rises.

GOLD FEVER

Gold fever harks back to the California Gold Rush 160 years ago but continues to this day. Panning for gold, a practice where a pan the size of a pie plate is used to sift through river sediment to discover gold nuggets, has seen a modern-day resurgence in California near the original gold rush sites. An estimated 12.5 million ounces of gold have been extracted from the Canadian Klondike region since the discovery of gold there in 1896.

This love affair with gold has had a lasting impact on American culture. Writers Jack London and Robert W. Service are two standout examples of authors who owe their careers to gold. Both became famous for works set amid the background of the late nineteenth-century gold rush, such as London's books *White Fang* and *To Build a Fire,* and Service's poems "The Shooting of Dan McGrew," "The Law of the Yukon," and "The Cremation of Sam McGhee." London actually participated in the Klondike Gold Rush and nearly died from scurvy due to the harsh conditions.

A HOT COMMODITY

Gold advocates say that since its discovery several thousand years ago, gold has never been valued at zero; instead, through the eons of time it has been sought after and treasured. The metal is still relatively scarce, with only about $5 trillion of mined gold existing in the world today. While the price of gold gyrates on the commodities exchanges in an epic battle between hard assets and paper assets, investor demand for the gold has reached monumental proportions. In an April 2009 news release, the World Gold Council proclaimed:

> Sustained investor interest in gold over the course of 2008 against a backdrop of the worst year on record for global stock markets and many other asset classes, helped push dollar demand for the safe haven asset to $102 billion, a 29 percent increase on year earlier levels. According to World Gold Council's ("WGC") Gold Demand Trends, identifiable gold demand in tonnage terms rose 4 percent on previous year levels to 3,659 tonnes. As shares on stock markets around the world lost an estimated $14 trillion in value, identifiable investment demand for gold, which incorporates exchange traded funds (ETFs) and bars and coins, was 64 percent higher in 2008 than in 2007, equivalent to an additional inflow of $US15 billion. Over the year as a whole, the gold price averaged $872, up 25 percent from $695 in 2007.
>
> The most striking trend across the year was the reawakening of investor interest in the holding of physical gold. Demand for bars and coins rose 87 percent over the year with shortages reported across many parts of the globe.

The Gold Council's press release also contained a litany of other superlatives:

A striking and glittering 1932 Saint-Gaudens Double Eagle $20 gold piece. *Photo courtesy of the Numismatic Guaranty Corporation (NGC)*

- Jewelry demand up 11 percent in dollar terms at almost $US60 billion for the whole year, but down 11 percent in tonnage terms at 2,138 tonnes.

- Industrial demand in 2008 was another casualty of the global economic turmoil down 7 percent to 430 tonnes from 461 tonnes in 2007.

- Total demand remained very strong in the fourth quarter of 2008, up 26 percent on the same period last year at 1,036 tonnes or $26.5 billion in value terms.

- The biggest source of growth in demand for gold in Q4 was investment. Identifiable investment demand reached 399 tonnes, up from 141 tonnes in Q4 2007, a rise of 182 percent. The main source of this increase was net retail investment, which rose 396 percent from 61 tonnes in Q4 2007 to 304 tonnes in Q4 2008.

- The most dramatic surge was in Europe, where bar and coin demand increased from just 9 tonnes in Q4 2007 to 114 tonnes in Q4 2008, a 1,170 percent increase.

- Total demand in India, the world's largest gold market, in the fourth quarter was up 84 percent in tonnage terms, led by a very strong 107 percent rise in jewelry demand.

- Total gold demand in Greater China in Q4 was resilient to the global turmoil. Total off-take was up 21 percent on the same period last year, with investment the main contributor to growth but jewelry demand also holding up well.

- Demand in the Middle East in Q4 2008 was up 1 percent relative to the previous year's levels, with the strong growth in the bar and coin market (up 139 percent) offset by 7 percent decline in jewelry demand, which makes up 90 percent of the market in this region.

- In the United States, the deteriorating economic conditions produced a mixed result for gold demand. Fourth quarter jewelry demand was down 35 percent as consumer spending plummeted. In stark contrast, demand for gold bars and coins rocketed by 370 percent in Q4, representing 35 tonnes of gold.

- Gold supply in Q4 was up 5 percent relative to the previous year's levels and year-on-year, declined 1 percent. Slightly lower mine production, higher levels of scrap, and lower levels of gold producer de-hedging were partly offset by lower net central bank sales in Q4 2008, which totaled 71 tonnes, down from 97 tonnes in Q4 2007.

SOME TEARS FOR TWO TIERS

A stunning example of a 1799 Draped Bust Heraldic Eagle $10 gold piece. *Photo courtesy of the Numismatic Guaranty Corporation (NGC)*

The resurgence of gold's popularity as a safe-haven asset has created a two-tiered gold market. The spot price has traded at one level, while the physical price for gold has traded at a higher level due to strong demand for gold coins and bullion. The primary reason for this is that in surveying today's scarred economic landscape, investors have lost confidence in fiat money and other paper assets. Demand has been strong enough to lift the premium of a bullion gold coin by more than 7 percent above the spot price.

Extremely strong demand in the crack-out arena, where a graded coin has the chance to grade even higher, has helped boost the price level 10 percent or more above the COMEX (commodities division of the New York Mercantile Exchange) spot price for twenty dollar uncirculated gold coins from the late nineteenth and early twentieth centuries. These particular coins have become popular with investors because they offer both a modest collectible premium due to their age as well as nearly an ounce of gold—not to mention the potential to crack the coin out and resubmit the coin to a grading service for a potentially higher grade.

Even before the crack-out boom for gold pieces set in, investors had been paying modest premiums, somewhat more than melt value, for collectible-quality Liberty and Saint-Gaudens double eagles in barely uncirculated condition. Gold bullion coins such as the American Eagle, the Canadian Maple Leaf, and the South African Krugerrand are, in 2009, bringing premiums of more than 5 percent to almost 10 percent—well above normal levels.

As the bar chart below illustrates, an ounce of gold can command different prices in different forms. Speculators who have been purchasing MS-63 Liberty or Saint-Gaudens twenty dollar gold pieces containing about an ounce of gold have been paying premiums of more than 10 percent to gain some collectible value along with the market value of the gold itself. On the other hand, speculators in the futures market have been paying lower prices. Is it manipulation in the paper gold market (a controversial theory held by some that the price of paper gold has been artificially suppressed by the government and major banks), or simply a matter of strong demand for physical gold? Other investors are paying smaller premiums over futures for bullion gold pieces. Bullion tends to cost a bit less than twenty dollar gold pieces, but is more vulnerable to swings in the futures market.

■ THE COST FOR AN OUNCE OF GOLD CAN VARY

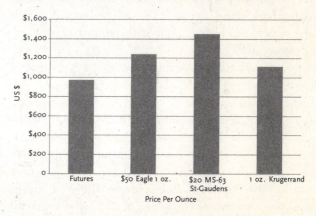

The Cost for an Ounce of Gold Can Vary. *Data from recent market and dealer quotes*

On the other hand, more expensive collector gold coins that had been selling for more than twenty-five thousand dollars dropped precipitously before gold recovered in early 2009. These examples show normally staid pricing trends that went "ballistic," as one dealer put it, in 2008 when gold slumped from its highs above one thousand dollars. Drops in gold coins valued at more than ten thousand dollars have been as much as 25 percent.

WORLDWIDE MINING TRENDS

South Africa continues to lay claim as the nation where the most gold is extracted from the ground, despite serious problems with electricity supply. According to the World Gold Council data (as of 2006, the most recent data available), South Africa produced 292 metric tons of gold, or 12 percent of the world total. In comparison, the United States produced 252 metric tons and China produced 247 metric tons.

The Grasberg mine in Indonesia, a joint venture of Rio Tinto and Freeport-McMoRan Copper & Gold, has emerged as the world's largest gold-producing mine, with production of over 114 metric tons of gold.

The second-largest gold-producing mine is the Yanachocha mine in Peru, at fourteen thousand feet above sea level in the Andes Mountains, where 203 metric tons were produced in 2006.

Extracting gold may seem as simple as building mine shafts deep beneath the earth, finding a mother lode of gold, digging the nuggets out, sending it up the mine elevator, melting the nuggets down, and then pouring glowing yellowish liquefied metal into forms that cool down into gold bars. But it's a far, far more complicated process—a costly one at that—and one that can bring out the darkest of human nature.

Learning from the Bre-X Scandal

Bre-X Minerals is a corporate name that will live in infamy in the annals of gold mining and investing. The mining company was responsible for the worst scandal ever in the industry—an egregious example of just how complicated matters can become when the dishonest are given free reign and investors looking to make a fast buck forget the age-old adage that if it seems too good to be true, it probably is. Bre-X shares bubbled to a market capitalization of $6 billion in 1995 until it was discovered that there was nothing behind the glitzy promise of "gold in them thar hills." The "hills" in this case were what was promised to be an entire mountain full of millions of ounces of gold in Indonesia's Borneo jungle region, known collectively as the Busang deposit. It's a story that inspired five books about the high-stakes risk, the all or nothing exploration, deceit, and even allegations of murder involved. It entangled the biggest names on Wall Street and in the mining industry.

The saga of Bre-X dates back to 1993, when the junior mining company, run by chairman David Walsh, bought the hitherto ignored Busang site and proceeded to report ever-increasing gold deposit estimates, despite reports of little gold in previous years. By 1997 the estimates topped a record 200 million ounces. Investors had struck it rich, or so they thought. With each higher estimate, Bre-X shares rallied, reaching an ultimate crescendo of more than $250 per share from penny stock status just a few short years before.

But plot complications set in. The lofty claims of Bre-X were eventually challenged by a corporate partner who found little gold in ground-test samples. The mountain of lies quickly unraveled. When mining giant Freeport-McMoRan Copper & Gold entered the fray in March 1997 and did its own testing, it found virtually no gold or gold particles from the Busang site that were different from gold particle samples provided by Bre-X. It turned out that previous core samples of the earth supposedly taken in the Busang region had been falsified, and that the gold samples used to perpetuate the fraud weren't even samples of the type of gold found in the region. The claims made early in Bre-X's history that ore was evident at the earth's surface were never borne out as natives who panned for gold in the waterways of the region never found any gold. Disclosure of the dead deposits sent Bre-X shares tumbling on Canadian exchanges: They lost half their value in the space of a day, and 90 percent in the space of a few more weeks.

Just two days after the samples were disclosed, company geologist Michael de Guzman was summoned to compare notes with Freeport, but on his way to the meeting, he apparently stepped off, or fell out of, a helicopter flying at over six hundred feet to his death, deep into the jungle below. His demise was ruled a suicide.

Wall Street firms were virtually useless in predicting this disaster. At the end of 2006 (just months before the Bre-X collapse), now-defunct Lehman Brothers was touting the virtues of Bre-X, calling the company's gold discovery, "enormous." Just a month before the shares collapsed, J.P. Morgan, in its role as advisor, featured a Bre-X geologist heralding the size of the gold deposit on a conference call with investors.

Much like the scandals of today, billions of dollars in shareholder equity was erased. And much like the scandals of today, red flags were ignored and skullduggerous deeds were allowed to fester and proliferate until it was too late. The founder of the company died in 1999. Other promoters of the company were amazingly never charged, or were even exonerated of securities fraud charges in Canadian courts.

The Bre-X case is also instructive on another front: Gold generally does not pop out of the ground for quick and easy discovery and mining. Recovering gold involves blood, sweat, and tears—and if not sweat, then bearing the freezing temperatures of the northernmost reaches of the world.

SEWER GOLD

Why spend billions of dollars to mine for gold when far more than trace amounts have been found in sewage? In Japan, where sewage is often incinerated, the leftover ash has contained pure gold. Press reports say sewer districts have retrieved nearly two kilograms of gold per metric ton of ash from the sludge they incinerate. That's almost fifty times what miners extract from Japan's Hishikari Mine—one of the world's top gold mines. The gold primarily comes from plants manufacturing high-technology instruments that contain gold.

As unappetizing as the sewage story is, it drives home a point: Gold is something not to be wasted, and little of it *has* been wasted. According to the World Gold Council, "since all the gold that has ever been mined still exists aboveground, it's possible that the jewelry you're wearing, or the gold coin in your possession, could be comprised of gold that was mined in prehistoric times!" Now it can also be stated that the gold may have spent some time soaking in wastewater treatment systems.

A GOLD SHORTAGE IMPACTS THE MINT

Volatility in the metals market has caught up with the U.S. Mint. In January 2009 the Mint announced a new pricing structure to enable it to respond more quickly to price changes in the spot market. The Mint also raised premiums on the various coins that it markets in response to price increases in raw metals.

During 2008, the Mint suspended sales of gold products for periods of time. In August, sales of Gold Eagle bullion coins were suspended for two weeks and then resumed on a rationed basis, a move that caught many off guard. The Mint confessed that "the unprecedented demand for American Eagle gold one-ounce bullion coins necessitates our allocating these coins among the authorized purchasers on a weekly basis until we are able to meet demand."

In September 2008, the Mint suspended sales of American Buffalo gold bullion coins. Sales were resumed after a month, but only to clear remaining inventory. The Mint announced that its inventories were depleted—again it could not keep up with demand. A month later, the Mint was still struggling and issued an update, saying it would focus only on producing American Eagle one-ounce gold and silver coins. In November 2008, the Mint announced plans to slash its offerings by 60 percent.

The Mint News blog (*http://mintnewsblog.blogspot.com*) called the cut in product offerings "shocking." Blogger Michael Zielinski reported: "[The cuts include] a large array of bullion-related products, eliminating nearly all American Buffalo Gold offerings, nearly all Platinum Eagle offerings, and the fractional uncirculated Gold Eagle offerings. This is a major retrenchment from the array of 'collectible' bullion coins currently offered by the U.S. Mint. Other discontinued products are related to the ending of the 50 State Quarters Program. The remainder of discontinuations are for less popular offerings [such as] Presidential dollar series and some other fringe products like collectible spoons."

Later that month, the Mint announced that it would be delaying a variety of bullion products due to a shortage of gold.

As of this writing, given the variety of initiatives announced in recent months, the supply of coins being generated appears to have stabilized, though further demand for gold and silver in futures and bullion markets could make the situation difficult again even for the U.S. Mint.

The Mint has also announced a new return policy and is now giving buyers only seven days to return merchandise due to quickly changing market prices.

WAYS TO INVEST

As with most metals, you can invest in gold by buying the physical ("hard") asset in bullion or coin form or buying an exchange-traded fund. For gold investors the vehicle of choice for many has been the Gold Exchange Traded Fund, known as GLD. There are pros and cons to investing in precious metals ETFs—the main downside being that you do not own any gold or silver. (See chapter 7, Value Trends in Silver, for more information about ETFs.)

Gold has its ups and downs, like any other investment. An investment in bullion exposes an investor to greater sensitivity to moves in the spot price as opposed to buying late nineteenth and early twentieth century gold coins, which gives investors a bit more insulation from daily spot price fluctuation because of the added collectibles value of the older coins. A fifty dollar move in the spot price of gold won't automatically change an older coin's value, while the bullion price will move in tandem with the spot price, even if it has been trading at a higher premium in the two-tiered market scenario.

A $50 gold bullion coin produced by the U.S. Mint. *Image courtesy of the U.S. Mint*

MAKING POTENTIALLY BIG MONEY IN CRACK-OUTS

There's a form of coin arbitrage that has become wildly popular, and all it takes is an initial outlay of cash to purchase a coin and the ability to pick out the right one. The term that's used to describe this practice is "cracking out." It's a process in which a buyer seeks out an under-graded coin, carefully cracks it out of its protective holder, and resubmits it to a grading service with the goal of receiving a higher grade.

The potential gains are enormous. For example, a 1915 Saint-Gaudens Double Eagle graded MS-64 by the Professional Coin Grading Service (PCGS) is worth $6,300 as of this writing. In MS-65, just one grade higher, the coin commands twenty-six thousand dollars.

Late nineteenth- and early twentieth-century Saint-Gaudens Double Eagles—twenty dollar gold pieces that contain nearly an ounce of the yellow metal—have been especially popular crack-out selections because they offer so much more bang for the buck than less-valuable coins like silver Morgan dollars—though the right Morgan getting an upgrade can still yield a handsome profit.

The practice is easier said than done, however, and should be attempted only by an expert with a keen eye for under-graded coins. Someone who isn't skilled—and also not careful—may end up choosing an over-graded coin, sending it to a grading service, and receiving a lower, money-losing grade. Or, they might damage the coin when they crack it out of the holder.

There is no set rule on what type of coin makes a good crack-out candidate. Morgan silver dollars might be a better choice for a speculator who has had more experience with them. A primary key to success in the crack-out game is to seek out coins that were graded a decade or more in the past, when grading standards were stricter. The standards of today increase the odds that an older graded coin could be a winning crack-out candidate, though there is no guarantee. On the flip side, what may have been desirable to coin graders a decade ago may be less desirable now and you could get your coin returned with the same grade as before it was cracked out.

Crack-out players must be at the top of their game in order to be consistent winners. Often, someone looking for a crack-out upgrade must resubmit the same coin to a grading service several times before hitting pay dirt. Coin-grading services don't take their responsibilities lightly. When it awards a high grade to a coin, a grading service is putting its name on the line and potentially creating instant wealth for the coin's owner.

▪ 1908-D NO-MOTTO MS-64 SAINT-GAUDENS DOUBLE EAGLE

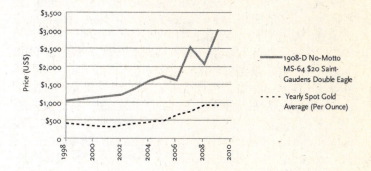

Time and Rarity Are on the Side of Coin Collectors. The 1908-D No-Motto $20 Saint-Gaudens is an example of a coin that has risen in price sharply independently of its intrinsic value. As this chart illustrates, even as gold cratered, the coin's value continued to increase.

BUYING COINS ON TV OR OVER THE PHONE

The quickest advice from coin advocates is to hang up and tune out. Unless the coins being touted on television shopping channels are certified and authenticated by a professional grading service such as PCGS or NGC, you are relying only on the subjective grading claims and dubious authority of guests and hosts. The deception can be subtle. In one TV ad, a gold huckster advertises that the buyer will receive a Morgan dollar in "very fine" to "BU" condition. That could be anything from a beautiful brilliant uncirculated (BU) coin to a very worn down "very fine" specimen. The buyer is likely to end up with a well-worn coin that would have little, if any, collectible value.

OBAMA COINS—SENTIMENTAL VALUE, BUT NO REAL VALUE

As coins grab the attention of more people, a more dubious trend is taking place: the proliferation of unofficially manufactured coins from companies that put the word "Mint" in their names, but offer products with little to no real monetary or collectible value. As an example, Barack Obama coin offerings continue to make the rounds, whether on late-night television infomercials or on the Web. Buyer, beware!

The Professional Numismatists Guild (PNG) furnished this guidance on the Obama coins: "All of the items we've seen offered so far on television and online are merely political mementos that certainly may be enjoyable as a keepsake, but typically will have little or no resale value later in the mainstream numismatic market. Privately-produced items are not legal-tender U.S. coins. In cases where a marketer has altered an actual U.S. coin after it left the Mint, such as putting a sticker with Obama's picture on it, knowledgeable collectors usually consider that to be merely defacing the coin."

The U.S. Mint issued its own, more in-depth statement alerting the general public that the Barack Obama Presidential one-dollar coins and other similar coins bearing images of Obama are *not* U.S. Mint products and are not endorsed or authorized by the Mint. The Mint added that it does not endorse this or any alterations of official Mint coins.

As a general rule of thumb, ordering coins via infomercials and commercials is a proposition that is fraught with risk. Be careful.

CONFISCATION: CAN IT HAPPEN AGAIN?

With a proclamation from President Franklin Roosevelt in 1933 (see full text of the presidential order in Appendix B), gold bullion ownership became illegal. Americans were forced to turn in their non-collectible gold.

New York City lawyer and noted coin expert and author David Ganz doubts gold will be confiscated as it was during the Great Depression, but the means to do it still exists. That has impacted purchasing habits by some investors. The following is an interview conducted with Ganz.

J.K.: FDR did it, so is it possible that another occupant of the White House may move to have gold confiscated?

Ganz: It's very possible because the same basis that FDR used in 1933, which was the Trading With the Enemy Act of 1917, is still on the books. It authorizes the president, in the event of a declaration of an emergency, to seize gold and a series of other metals.

J.K.: It was strictly gold in 1933. What other metals could be involved?

Ganz: It could be silver, it could be platinum and any other metal the president deems in the national interest.

J.K.: How would a modern-day gold confiscation be undertaken?

Ganz: Pretty much the same as it did during the Roosevelt administration. An executive order would be issued by the president, though it could be done by the Treasury secretary under different statutes and methodology, but it would be the same. It would direct that gold coins be turned in under which the government would agree to redeem the gold coin at their face value.

J.K.: Would the American population cooperate? There are a lot of enraged people out there already.

Ganz: I think there were a lot of enraged people during the 1930s when this happened. Some of them went to court saying that it was illegal, some of them went to court saying it was unconstitutional and those issues were all litigated very successfully with the government prevailing in its view.

J.K.: How would the U.S. look on the world stage having to confiscate gold from its citizens?

Ganz: I doubt seriously we would undertake this by ourselves. You would probably see a number of the members of the G-20 act simultaneously so that you didn't see people in one jurisdiction shifting their assets to another jurisdiction.

J.K.: What reasons would the government cite for confiscation?

Ganz: Legally they wouldn't need to do anything more than to make the basic finding that the Trading With the Enemy Act requires that essentially it's in the national interest for this to take place.

J.K.: What would this do to the value of coins that collectors would be allowed to keep?

Ganz: This might be a good thing for collectors. What happens is that the price would go up, which is what happened in 1933. Gold went up by 59 percent.

The impact of FDR's gold confiscation lasted for more than five decades. Gold bullion coins would not be minted until an act of Congress in 1985 made it possible. (See Appendix B for the full text of the Gold Bullion Coin Act of 1985.)

A WORD ABOUT SENDING YOUR GOLD THROUGH THE MAIL FOR CASH

Don't do it!

Much time is spent in this book discussing the purchase of gold. Supposing you wish to sell it? It cannot be stressed too vehemently that you should avoid "convenient" television buying services that will take your gold sight unseen. You'll be in much better hands taking your coins and scrap gold to an ANA-certified coin dealer.

Recently we've seen a proliferation of advertisements promising near-instant money for gold, in which individuals wishing to sell their excess gold jewelry are encouraged to send it in for a fast turnaround check. Complaints about the amounts of such checks have steadily increased since the ads began appearing. Before sending your gold to anyone—or, for that matter, buying gold, get a local opinion on how much it's worth. Attorneys general have been circulating tips on how to avoid being taken.

Here are some of these tips:

- **Get an appraisal.** Have your gold assessed by an accredited appraiser or a neutral jeweler or collector to find the accurate weight and gold content.

- **Find a reputable buyer.** This could include checking out names with the Better Business Bureau or determining whether the person who's buying your coin is a member of the American Numismatic Association (ANA).

- **Beware of scams.** Scam artists are also tapping into the gold rush. They're using phone solicitations, Web sites, direct mail, and Tupperware-style gold parties to trick consumers into selling their gold for less than its true value. Some mail-in companies promise consumers cash in exchange for sending their unwanted gold jewelry and coins. If you mail your gold, you risk losing it completely or not getting a fair price for it.

- **Determine the fair markup price.** Check the commodities markets for that day's spot price. Market prices are based on pure twenty-four-karat gold, so the higher the karat, the more valuable it is. Gold less than twenty-four karats is discounted proportionately: eighteen karats is 75 percent pure gold, fourteen karats is 58 percent, and ten-karat gold is 41.7 percent pure. The scrap price is based on the value of the metal alone and doesn't reflect the craftsmanship or antique value of the item.

- **Shop around.** Get at least three estimates from different jewelers. Ask jewelers how much they offer for pure gold, how they calculate the value of a gold item, and what percentage commission they charge (typically about 10 percent).

- **Consider the consequences.** When you melt your gold jewelry, you lose all of its collectible (and sentimental) value. Your antique jewelry may be worth more than just its weight in gold. Think twice before you melt it.

One company, Cash4Gold, attracted attention by purchasing a Super Bowl ad at the start of 2009. A quick check using a search engine such as Google and the keyword "cash4gold" will retrieve not only the Web site of the company, but a host of complaints on consumer bulletin boards and by a variety of bloggers. One online skeptic posed an excellent question on Answers.com, asking, "Who would give their gold to a stranger without pre-appraisal? I Just don't get it." That's something everyone should ask before shipping gold in the mail.

GOLD FORECASTS: AN OVERDONE RALLY?

In the space of a little more than a decade, gold has gone from being the Rodney Dangerfield of the financial world—getting no respect—to attracting a broad amount of interest. While base metals and other precious metals are not directly tied to the movement of gold, the metals universe in general takes its cues from the health of the very actively traded gold market.

A review of natural resources "north of the border," once home to the thousands of Klondike gold prospectors of 1899 and 1900, seems an appropriate starting point when discussing gold forecasts.

Toronto-based BMO (Bank of Montreal) Capital Markets analyst Bert Malek thinks a perfect storm would benefit gold. Malek calls gold the "ultimate money," saying that it is "money, a financial asset, and a physical metal all bundled into a yellow brick or wafer." Gold, he says, "morphs into different purposes" and is seen as a mitigator of risk. "There appears to be traditional flight-to-quality buying as investors seek the safety of physical bullion," Malek says. "Gold could easily top one thousand dollars in the coming year."

But Malek offers the caveat that as gold rises even as the dollar attracts safe-haven interest, "it is possible that gold could re-test $850 per ounce before trending back up." Malek also thinks hyperinflation is not on the financial menu at this time. "We're not expecting inflation Armageddon," but notes that inflation could pick up and that "gold is usually twelve to eighteen months ahead of actual inflation."

This begs the question: Is the gold rally sustainable? Says Malek: "It's definitely a long-term bull market with three thousand dollars an ounce talk, crazy stuff."

But he warns that if confidence comes back into the overall financial system and inflation doesn't spin out of control, then "gold is vulnerable." He says investors shouldn't chase the market, but buy on corrections.

$2,011 Gold by 2011

American Numismatic Association president Barry Stuppler sees gold at $2,011 by 2011.

"I feel very strongly we're seeing a tremendous amount of new buying coming into the market. This new buying is not the same buyers who were around a year ago who were looking for capital appreciation and diversification. Most people I'm talking to now are interested in purchasing gold because they're afraid of holding currency with the trillions of dollars, yen, and euro that are being issued by various governments around the world in various bailout packages," says Stuppler.

Stuppler adds, "My projection, I made it June of last year, was that we would see gold at $2,011 by the end of 2011. At this point, considering what's happening with the stimulus packages, it [gold's rise to $2,011] could happen before 2011. We're seeing the gold market react to a deterioration not just in the dollar, but global currencies and the only safe harbor as investor that you have to protect against the collapse of the buying power of currency is to have gold."

Alaron Trading's Phil Flynn is cautious. Flynn, Alaron's vice president of market research, says "the reason why people are running to gold is that they fear hyperinflation. Their trust in the Treasury . . . is diminished; they don't trust we're going to get out of this situation."

Stuppler says buyers should be diversified. "I would say have some of the gold bullion coins and have some of the numismatic investment coins because right now the buyers who are coming in are concerned about a lot of things because one of the major issues out there, and I don't think it's going to happen, is possible confiscation of gold. This has been in a lot of newsletters and it's been fueling demand for a lot of the non-bullion products like the twenty-dollar gold Saint-Gaudens."

CITIGROUP IS BULLISH

"Frankly, we're surprised that gold is not already at two thousand dollars an ounce," declared Citigroup analysts John H. Hill and Graham Wark, who in late 2008 made an eye-opening and gutsy call on the price of gold. Brokerage firms bullish on gold have maintained higher but fairly tight trading ranges for gold—but not Hill and Wark.

"Gold appears to be entering a powerful new phase of investment demand tied to safe-haven and monetization themes," they stated in their report.

"We have been surprised that gold has been so heretofore quiet, and have expected a much stronger and more immediate response to the government takeover of GSE [Government Sponsored Enterprises]/mortgage insurance entities and broker-deal bankruptcies," they wrote. "It is notable that hard-core gold bugs have been proven correct in the decade-long contention that an overwhelmingly vast and complex pool of nested financial derivatives would ultimately result in cascading defaults and ruin for major portions of the banking system."

"Our sense is that gold has been temporarily depressed by a series of ephemeral, short-term trading dynamics that served to mask strong physical off-take in what is ultimately a tiny market," the analysts said. "We continue to regard it as a barometer in the grand battle between hard assets and paper assets."

Hill and Wark emphasized the safe-haven qualities of gold in their bullish forecast, especially during a deep and protracted worldwide recession. "Gold and precious metals would prove to be one of the few safe havens for capital preservation," they said, "particularly given likely low to negative real interest rates in such a scenario. In this case, we would expect gold to double or triple from more current levels."

A more likely macro outcome involves slow growth accompanied by the monetization and socialization of derivatives losses," the analysts said. "Actions such as the U.S. takeover of GSE/mortgage and insurance entities and lending/guarantees to derivatives-laden banks, replicated globally, are likely to act to the detriment of paper currencies relative to hard assets and gold."

"As we have maintained for months, gold seems to be badly mispriced and a uniformly dour sentiment for industrial metals and coal," Hill and Wark said. "We remain positive on gold, based on a mix of macro and supply-demand drivers."

"The forces that have propelled gold for the past five years are firmly in place, and policy prescriptions for the credit crisis seem powerfully and uniformly reflationary. Prices are up in the euro, yen, and rupees, a crucial credibility test. Gold is below constant-dollar peaks of eighteen hundred to three thousand dollars per ounce and has lagged bulk/base metals since the 2001 trough. Appreciation remains muted relative to other metals and oil. Ultimately, gold is a small market with motivated Indian/Asian and petrodollar-fueled buyers."

The analysts forecast that the gold price will go higher through 2010 and maintain year-average forecasts of $950 to one thousand dollars per ounce.

UBS Is Bullish

UBS sees gold rising as its status as a safe-haven investment becomes more embraced around the world.

"Purchases of physical gold have jumped over the past six months as investors' fears about the current financial crisis and the possible outcomes from government efforts to support banks and economies have intensified," according to UBS strategist John Reade.

Reade and his team have set 2009 and 2010 average price targets of one thousand dollars and nine hundred dollars, respectively. UBS says demand for gold could double from 2007, but then gradually decline in 2010.

Merrill Lynch Is Bullish

Merrill Lynch's chief investment officer for Global Wealth Management in Europe Middle East and Africa (EMEA) region, Gary Dugan, says gold could reach fifteen hundred dollars per ounce in the next year.

"We have never seen such a rush to buy gold. It's bringing in security and it's still affordable," Dugan said.

Dugan cites a variety of factors favoring gold, including shaken confidence in currencies and declining gold production even as demand rises.

Political realities also are likely to negatively impact the dollar, he says. "That's when people will begin to realize that President Obama's policies are not having the desired impact," he said.

"The rich are asking for gold bars, as they are worried over how the economy would behave this year," according to Dugan, who adds that gold is being favored while paper investments and proxies are being shunned.

Gold has long battled with the thousand dollar an ounce barrier—rising to that level and then pulling back. Given the multi-trillion dollar budget deficits and the multi-trillion dollar bailout costs we're seeing now, gold has a better chance than ever of breaking through one thousand dollars and remaining above that level, if not climbing even higher.

9
VALUE TRENDS IN PLATINUM

When platinum was trading at more than $2,200 an ounce in early 2008 auto repair shops were being approached by people who were looking to take used catalytic converters off the hands of the shops—presenting their service as a favor. Platinum, palladium, and the super-rare rhodium are metals used in the converter to cause chemical reactions under high heat in order to reduce the toxicity of auto emissions. Repair-shop employees who agreed to part with the converters may not have realized that they were giving away devices worth a few hundred dollars or more apiece due to the metallic content.

Platinum is the rarest of all precious metals. While silver is known as "the poor man's gold," platinum's sobriquet is "the rich man's gold." (The recording industry recognizes the special value of platinum: While a record that has gone "gold" is quite the success at five hundred thousand copies sold, a recording that's gone platinum signifies sales of one million albums.)

The U.S. Geologic Survey (USGS) defines platinum this way: "Naturally occurring platinum and platinum-rich alloys have been known for a long time. The Spaniards named the metal 'platina,' or little silver, when they first encountered it in Colombia. They regarded platinum as an unwanted impurity in the silver they were mining."

Today platinum, which is more rare and harder to find than gold or silver, is anything but a nuisance. It's used in the refining of crude oil and the production of high-octane gasoline, and more than 59 percent of platinum's use is in the auto industry, even in the current climate of stunted auto sales. Platinum's industrial uses are also key in the chemicals industry, according to the USGS: "Platinum, platinum alloys, and iridium are used as crucible materials for the growth of single crystals, especially oxides. The chemical industry uses a significant amount of either platinum or a platinum-rhodium alloy catalyst in the form of gauze to catalyze the partial oxidation of ammonia to yield nitric oxide, which is the raw material for fertilizers, explosives, and nitric acid."

About 7 million ounces of platinum are taken out of the ground each year compared with around 80 million ounces of gold and more than 500 million ounces of silver. The trajectory for auto-related demand had been ever higher (with a few bumps) since catalytic converters were installed in cars starting with the 1975 model year in the United States. Although automakers are currently struggling for survival, stringent federal anti-pollution requirements for future model years will continue to support platinum demand.

The industrial demand for platinum is the reason why, when the price floor gave way for commodities by mid-2008, platinum cratered more in line with nonfinancial commodities and failed to hold up as well as gold or silver.

A platinum bullion coin produced by the U.S. Mint. *Image courtesy of the U.S. Mint*

Nearly 25 percent of the platinum that's mined today is used for jewelry, though demand for jewelry use is actually down nearly 50 percent from 2000 as a consequence of higher platinum prices. At the start of this century platinum was trading at $450 an ounce. Today China reigns as the leading platinum jewelry market.

South African Mining Woes

South African mines generate nearly 80 percent of the world's platinum supply (Russia is the second largest producer at 10 percent of world output), with nearly 90 percent of that output coming from the Western Bushveld region of the country, west of the capital of Pretoria. Mining is a dangerous enterprise for those who are brave enough to go down the shafts each day. In 2008, 168 workers died in mine-related accidents, according to local media accounts. Extracting platinum requires deep mining of a mile or more and the processing of over ten tons of ore to yield just one pure ounce of the "white metal." With the processing being done miles underground, miners endure temperatures of 120 degrees to accomplish their task.

It has clearly been a raucous time for the entire mining industry in South Africa. Beyond supply and demand, the price of platinum is also greatly impacted by mine closures due to accidents and strikes and by the volatility in prices of other metals. From May 2008 to October 2008, platinum nosedived from more than $2,200 an ounce to $771 an ounce in October—a drop that could give any industry cardiac arrest. The price surged to $2,200 as commodities experienced a frenzy of buying by hedge funds and other speculators not wanting to be left behind; however, when it became all too apparent that world economies were contracting, investors flocked to dollars and dollar equivalents as a safe haven, leaving platinum—whose industrial uses make it dependent on global growth—hard hit by October 2008.

The outlook for platinum is not entirely bleak. Despite fluctuations over the past year or so, even at its recent low point in 2008 the price of platinum was still roughly double its 1998 price of about $370 per ounce. And mining companies have been able to put a floor under the price of platinum since late 2008 by implementing production cutbacks—eliminating thousands of jobs and lowering output in South Africa. These actions, along with a rebound in commodities prices, have caused the metal's price to move back above $1,100 per ounce. Demand from China has also increased, helping to push platinum higher. The outlook for platinum could even become quite rosy if the automotive industry were to recover and demand were to pick up for antipollution exhaust devices.

There will be other problems for these mines to confront, including a shortage of skilled labor—a longstanding problem in South Africa—when hiring resumes. As an additional challenge, contract negotiations under way between mining companies and workers show a wide chasm on wages, with miners seeking a 15 percent wage increase and companies offering no more than a 5 percent increase at this writing. Limits on electricity generation in South Africa is yet another potential roadblock to output and a source of worry for investors.

INVESTORS LOVE U.S. PLATINUM BULLION COINS

The history of U.S. Mint–struck platinum bullion coins is brief. It was not until 1997 that the United States began offering platinum coins, doing so almost grudgingly due to availability of supply, in order to compete with platinum bullion coins being offered by other countries. The Mint has offered the American Eagle bullion coin in uncirculated and proof condition containing 99.95 percent pure platinum.

Despite the volatile price of platinum in 2008, demand for U.S. Mint–struck platinum American Eagle bullion soared to the point that the Mint was unable to cope with the rapidly fluctuating prices and was forced to suspend sales for periods of time in 2008 and 2009.

Platinum bullion coins are not for everyone. The price of the underlying metal has been volatile, making the investment too risky for some. However, platinum proponents feel the metal is actually priced too low given the amount of platinum production, at about 7 million ounces, versus 80 million ounces for gold in recent years. And though the performance of platinum has been unstable in the short term, over a ten-year stretch its price has nearly quadrupled.

EXCHANGE-TRADED PLATINUM NOTES

The UBS E-TRACS CMCI Long Platinum Total Return is a fund that tracks platinum through futures contracts that are closely correlated to the spot price of platinum. In the words of UBS, the fund "is designed to track the performance of the UBS Bloomberg CMCI Platinum Total Return, less investor fees. The CMCI Platinum TR measures the collateralized returns from a basket of platinum futures contracts. The commodity futures contracts are targeted for a constant maturity of three months."

This particular security trades under the ticker of PTM in the United States. Over a ten-year period (since 1998) CMCI boasts a total return of 988.75 percent and an annualized return of more than 25 percent. While PTM mimics the movement of platinum, it's entirely different from the famed GLD gold ETF in that PTM does not accumulate actual platinum as GLD does with its purchases of gold bullion.

PLATINUM FORECASTS

There's no doubt that while platinum is a volatile metal, over the long term (ten years or longer) it's a winner as an investment—a near fourfold increase in the price of platinum since 1999 speaks for itself. Platinum is also a bellwether for the metals group, due to its close ties with industrial demand, its use in jewelry, and its growing popularity as an investment vehicle. As in the past, platinum's rebound from October 2008 lows has led metals back into rally mode. A sure sign of a stronger bull market ahead for gold is to track the distance that platinum's trajectory takes it from gold. A good rule of thumb is that the larger the premium platinum has to gold, the stronger the rally is for both of the metals.

Metals and chemicals company Johnson Matthey says platinum could reach as high as $1,350 an ounce going into 2010. Its forecast seemed overly bullish early in 2009 when platinum was recovering from its 2008 plunge, but now (in mid-2009), with platinum hovering at about $1,150 an ounce, the Johnson forecast appears to be conservative.

However, there is the danger that platinum will become range-bound and stuck at around $1,200 an ounce due to ongoing world recession. Again, platinum is an industrial precious metals play, whereas gold is seen as a quasi-currency.

A poll of analysts by Reuters, as of this writing, shows the expectation for platinum to average $1,200 an ounce in 2010 with weakness in the auto sector weighing on prices. Reuters surveyed eighteen analysts.

With gold approaching one thousand dollars an ounce, if the analysts forecasting a plateau of $1,200 an ounce for platinum are correct, then the outlook for precious metals in general is somewhat bleak. However, with questions surrounding the credit worthiness of nations such as the United Kingdom and the United States, the accumulation of metals may be just getting started on a massive institutional level, which would leave some of the economic arguments against buying platinum in the dust.

APPENDIX A:

Coin Specifications

HALF CENTS

Diameter: 23.5 millimeters (about 15/16 of an inch)

Weight: 6.739 grams (0.238 ounce) in 1793–mid-1795, 5.443 grams (0.192 ounce) thereafter

Composition: 100 percent copper

Edge: Lettered TWO HUNDRED FOR A DOLLAR in 1793 and part of 1797, gripped in part of 1797, plain in all other cases

Designers: Henry Voight (1793), Robert Scot (1794–1808), John Reich (1809–1836), Christian Gobrecht (1840–1857)

LARGE CENTS

Diameter: 25–28 millimeters (about 15/16 of an inch–1 1/16 inches) in 1793, 27–30 millimeters (about 1 1/16–1 3/16 inches) in 1794, 28–29 millimeters (about 1 1/16–1 1/8 inches) thereafter

Weight: 13.478 grams (0.475 ounce) 1793–mid-1795; 10.886 grams (0.384 ounce) thereafter

Composition: 100 percent copper

Edge: Vine and bars in part of 1793, lettered ONE HUNDRED FOR A DOLLAR 1793–mid-1795, gripped in part of 1797, plain in all other cases

Designers: Henry Voight (1793 Chain and Wreath cents), Joseph Wright, Robert Scot, and John Smith Gardner (1793–1796 Liberty Cap), Robert Scot (1796–1807), John Reich (1808–1814 and 1816–1835), Christian Gobrecht (1835–1857)

FLYING EAGLE CENTS

Diameter: 19 millimeters (about 3/4 of an inch)

Weight: 4.666 grams (0.165 ounce)

Composition: 88 percent copper, 12 percent nickel

Edge: Plain

Designer: James B. Longacre

INDIAN HEAD CENTS

Diameter: 19 millimeters (about 3/4 of an inch)

Weight: 4.666 grams (0.165 ounce) 1859–mid-1864, 3.110 grams (0.110 ounce) mid-1864 and thereafter

Composition: 88 percent copper, 12 percent nickel 1859–mid-1864; 95 percent copper, 5 percent zinc and tin mid-1864 and thereafter

Edge: Plain

Designer: James B. Longacre

LINCOLN CENT

Diameter: 19 millimeters (about 3/4 of an inch)

Weight: 3.110 grams (0.110 ounce) 1909–mid-1982, except for 1943; 2.689 grams (0.095 ounce) in 1943; 2.5 grams (0.088 ounce) mid-1982 and thereafter

Composition: 95 percent copper, 5 percent zinc and tin 1909–mid-1962, except for 1943–1946; zinc-plated steel in 1943; 95 percent copper, 5 percent zinc 1944–1946, mid-1962–mid-1981; 97.5 percent zinc, 2.5 percent copper (copper-plated zinc) mid-1982 and thereafter

Edge: Plain

Designers: Victor D. Brenner (obverse 1909 to date, reverse 1909–1958), Frank Gasparro (reverse 1959 to date)

TWO-CENT PIECES

Diameter: 23 millimeters (about 9/10 of an inch)

Weight: 6.221 grams (0.219 ounce)

Composition: 95 percent copper, 5 percent zinc and tin

Edge: Plain

Designer: James B. Longacre

SILVER THREE-CENT PIECES

Diameter: 14 millimeters (about 9/16 of an inch)

Weight: 0.802 grams (0.028 ounce) 1851–1853, 0.746 grams (0.026 ounce) thereafter

Composition: 75 percent silver, 25 percent copper 1851–1853; 90 percent silver, 10 percent copper thereafter

Edge: Plain

Designer: James B. Longacre

NICKEL THREE-CENT PIECES

Diameter: 17.9 millimeters (about 7/10 of an inch)

Weight: 1.944 grams (0.069 ounce)

Composition: 75 percent copper, 25 percent nickel

Edge: Plain

Designer: James B. Longacre

HALF DIMES

Diameter: 16.5 millimeters (about 2/3 of an inch) 1792–1805, 15.5 millimeters (about 6/10 of an inch) thereafter

Weight: 1.348 grams (0.048 ounce) 1792–1836, 1.336 grams (0.047 ounce) 1837–mid-1853, 1.244 grams (0.044 ounce) mid-1853 and thereafter

Composition: 89.25 percent silver, 10.75 percent copper in 1792; 90 percent silver, 10 percent copper 1794–mid-1795; 89.25 percent silver, 10.75 percent copper mid-1795–1836; 90 percent silver, 10 percent copper 1837 and thereafter

Edge: Reeded

Designers: William Russell Birch (1792), Robert Scot (1794–1805)

COIN SPECIFICATIONS

SHIELD NICKELS

Diameter: 20.5 millimeters (about 13/16 of an inch)

Weight: 5 grams (0.176 ounce)

Composition: 75 percent copper, 25 percent nickel

Edge: Plain

Designer: James B. Longacre

LIBERTY HEAD NICKELS

Diameter: 21.2 millimeters (about 5/6 of an inch)

Weight: 5 grams (0.176 ounce)

Composition: 75 percent copper, 25 percent nickel

Edge: Plain

Designer: Charles E. Barber

BUFFALO HEAD NICKELS

Diameter: 21.2 millimeters (about 5/6 of an inch)

Weight: 5 grams (0.176 ounce)

Composition: 75 percent copper, 25 percent nickel

Edge: Plain

Designer: James E. Fraser

JEFFERSON NICKELS

Diameter: 21.2 millimeters (about 5/6 of an inch)

Weight: 5 grams (0.176 ounce)

Composition: 75 percent copper, 25 percent nickel 1938–mid-1942; 56 percent copper, 35 percent silver, 9 percent manganese mid-1942–1945

Edge: Plain

Designer: Felix Schlag

DRAPED BUST DIMES

Diameter: About 19 millimeters (3/4 of an inch)

Weight: 2.696 grams (0.095 ounce)

Composition: 89.25 percent silver, 10.75 percent copper

Edge: Reeded

Designer: Robert Scot

CAPPED BUST DIMES

Diameter: About 18.8 millimeters (3/4 of an inch) 1809–mid-1828; 18.5 millimeters (about 7/10 of an inch) mid-1828 and thereafter

Weight: 2.696 grams (0.095 ounce)

Composition: 89.25 percent silver, 10.75 percent copper 1809–1836; 90 percent silver, 10 percent copper 1837–l838

Edge: Reeded

Designer: John Reich

SEATED LIBERTY DIMES

Diameter: 17.9 millimeters (about 7/10 of an inch)

Weight: 2.673 grams (0.094 ounce) 1837–mid-1853; 2.488 grams (0.088 ounce) mid-1853–1872; 2.5 grams (0.088 ounce) 1873–1891

Composition: 90 percent silver, 10 percent copper

Edge: Reeded

Designer: Christian Gobrecht

BARBER DIMES

Diameter: 17.9 millimeters (about 7/10 of an inch)

Weight: 2.5 grams (0.088 ounce)

Composition: 90 percent silver, 10 percent copper

Edge: Reeded

Designer: Charles E. Barber

MERCURY DIMES

Diameter: 17.9 millimeters (about 7/10 of an inch)

Weight: 2.5 grams (0.088 ounce)

Composition: 90 percent silver, 10 percent copper

Edge: Reeded

Designer: Adolph A. Weinman

ROOSEVELT DIMES

Diameter: 17.9 millimeters (about 7/10 of an inch)

Weight: 2.5 grams (0.088 ounce) 1946–1964, 2.27 grams (0.080 ounce) 1965 to date

Composition: 90 percent silver, 10 percent copper 1946–1964; 75 percent copper, 25 percent nickel alloy bonded to pure copper core thereafter

Edge: Reeded

Designer: John R. Sinnock

TWENTY-CENT PIECES

Diameter: 22 millimeters (about 7/8 of an inch)

Weight: 5 grams (0.176 ounce)

Composition: 90 percent silver, 10 percent copper

Edge: Plain

Designer: William Barber

DRAPED BUST QUARTER-DOLLARS

Diameter: About 27.5 millimeters (1 1/12 inches)

Weight: 6.739 grams (0.238 ounce)

Composition: 89.25 percent silver, 10.75 percent copper

Edge: Reeded

Designer: Robert Scot

CAPPED BUST QUARTER-DOLLARS

Diameter: 27 millimeters (about 1 1/14 inches) 1815–1828, 24.3 millimeters (about 19/20 of an inch) 1831–1838

Weight: 6.739 grams (0.238 ounce) 1815–1836, 6.68 grams (0.236 ounce) 1837–1838

Composition: 89.25 percent silver, 10.75 percent copper 1815–1836; 90 percent silver, 10 percent copper 1837–1838

Edge: Reeded

Designer: John Reich

SEATED LIBERTY QUARTER-DOLLARS

Diameter: 24.3 millimeters (about 19/20 of an inch)

Weight: 6.68 grams (0.236 ounce) 1838–mid-1853, 6.221 grams (0.219 ounce) mid-1853–mid-1873; 6.25 grams (0.220 ounce) mid-1873–1891

Composition: 90 percent silver, 10 percent copper

Edge: Reeded

Designer: Christian Gobrecht

BARBER QUARTER-DOLLARS

Diameter: 24.3 millimeters (about 19/20 of an inch)

Weight: 6.25 grams (0.220 ounce)

Composition: 90 percent silver, 10 percent copper

Edge: Reeded

Designer: Charles Barber

STANDING LIBERTY QUARTER-DOLLARS

Diameter: 24.3 millimeters (about 19/20 of an inch)

Weight: 6.25 grams (0.220 ounce)

Composition: 90 percent silver, 10 percent copper

Edge: Reeded

Designer: Hermon A. MacNeil

WASHINGTON QUARTER-DOLLARS

Diameter: 24.3 millimeters (about 19/20 of an inch)

Weight: 6.25 grams (0.220 ounce) 1932–1964, 5.670 grams (0.200 ounce) 1965 to date

Composition: 90 percent silver, 10 percent copper 1932–1964, 75 percent copper, 25 percent nickel alloy bonded to pure copper core thereafter

Edge: Reeded

Designer: John Flanagan

*Note: State and Territorial quarter-dollars (minted 1999 to date) have the same specifications—except for the designer—as the Washington quarters of 1965–1998.

FLOWING HAIR HALF-DOLLARS

Diameter: About 32.5 millimeters (1 9/32 inches)

Weight: 13.48 grams (0.475 ounce)

Composition: 90 percent silver, 10 percent copper 1794–1795

Edge: Lettered FIFTY CENTS OR HALF A DOLLAR

Designer: Robert Scot

DRAPED BUST HALF-DOLLARS

Diameter: 32.5 millimeters (about 1 9/32 inches)

Weight: 13.48 grams (0.433 ounce)

Composition: 89.25 percent silver, 10.75 percent copper

Edge: Lettered FIFTY CENTS OR HALF A DOLLAR

Designer: Robert Scot

CAPPED BUST HALF-DOLLARS

Diameter: 32.5 millimeters (about 1 9/32 inches)

Weight: 13.48 grams (0.475 ounce)

Composition: 89.25 percent silver, 10.75 percent copper

Edge: Lettered FIFTY CENTS OR HALF A DOLLAR

Designer: John Reich

CAPPED BUST HALF-DOLLAR (REEDED EDGE)

Diameter: 30.6 millimeters (about 1 1/5 inches)

Weight: 13.48 grams (0.475 ounces) in 1836, 13.36 grams (0.471 ounce) 1837–1839

Composition: 89.25 percent silver, 10.75 percent copper in 1836; 90 percent silver, 10 percent copper 1837–1839

Edge: Reeded

Designer: Christian Gobrecht (adapted from the Capped Bust half-dollar design by John Reich)

SEATED LIBERTY HALF-DOLLARS

Diameter: 30.6 millimeters (about 1 1/5 inches)

Weight: 13.36 grams (0.471 ounce) 1839–mid-1853; 12.44 grams (0.439 ounce) mid-1853–mid-1873; 12.5 grams (0.402 ounce) mid-1873–1891

Composition: 90 percent silver, 10 percent copper

Edge: Reeded

Designer: Christian Gobrecht

BARBER HALF-DOLLARS

Diameter: 30.6 millimeters (about 1 1/5 inches)

Weight: 12.5 grams (0.441 ounce)

Composition: 90 percent silver, 10 percent copper

Edge: Reeded

Designer: Charles E. Barber

WALKING LIBERTY HALF-DOLLARS

Diameter: 30.6 millimeters (about 1 1/5 inches)

Weight: 12.5 grams (0.441 ounce)

Composition: 90 percent silver, 10 percent copper

Edge: Reeded

Designer: Adolph A. Weinman

FRANKLIN HALF-DOLLARS

Diameter: 30.6 millimeters (about 1 1/5 inches)

Weight: 12.5 grams (0.402 ounce)

Composition: 90 percent silver, 10 percent copper

Edge: Reeded

Designer: John R. Sinnock

KENNEDY HALF-DOLLARS

Diameter: 30.6 millimeters (about 1 1/5 inches)

Weight: 12.5 grams (0.441 ounce) in 1964; 11.5 grams (0.406 ounce) 1965–1970; 11.34 grams (0.400 ounce) 1971 to date

Composition: 90 percent silver, 10 percent copper in 1964; 40 percent silver, 60 percent copper 1965–1970 (80 percent silver, 20 percent copper alloy bonded to a 20.9 percent silver, 79.1 percent copper core); 75 percent copper, 25 percent nickel alloy bonded to pure copper core 1971 to date

Edge: Reeded

Designers: Gilroy Roberts (obverse) and Frank Gasparro (reverse)

FLOWING HAIR SILVER DOLLARS

Diameter: About 39–40 millimeters (1 9/16 inches)

Weight: 26.96 grams (0.951 ounce)

Composition: 90 percent silver, 10 percent copper

Edge: Lettered HUNDRED CENTS ONE DOLLAR OR UNIT

Designer: Robert Scot

DRAPED BUST SILVER DOLLARS

Diameter: 39.5 millimeters (about 1 5/9 inches)

Weight: 26.96 grams (0.951 ounce)

Composition: 89.25 percent silver, 10.75 percent copper

Edge: Lettered HUNDRED CENTS ONE DOLLAR OR UNIT

Designer: Robert Scot

GOBRECHT SILVER DOLLARS

Diameter: 39.5 millimeters (about 1 5/9 inches)

Weight: Issue of 1836 (first originals), 26.96 grams (0.951 ounce); issue of 1836 (second originals, struck in 1837) and 1838–1839, 26.73 grams (0.943 ounce)

Composition: 89.25 percent silver, 10.75 percent copper for 416-grain standard 1836 first originals; 90 percent silver, 10 percent copper for 412.5-grain standard 1836 second originals and 1838–1839

Edge: Plain in 1836, reeded in 1839

Designer: Christian Gobrecht

SEATED LIBERTY SILVER DOLLAR

Diameter: 38.1 millimeters (1 1/2 inches)

Weight: 26.73 grams (0.943 ounce)

Composition: 90 percent silver, 10 percent copper

Edge: Reeded

Designer: Christian Gobrecht

MORGAN SILVER DOLLARS

Diameter: 38.1 millimeters (1 1/2 inches)

Weight: 26.73 grams (0.943 ounce)

Composition: 90 percent silver, 10 percent copper

Edge: Reeded

Designer: George T. Morgan

PEACE SILVER DOLLARS

Diameter: 38.1 millimeters (1 1/2 inches)

Weight: 26.73 grams (0.943 ounce)

Composition: 90 percent silver, 10 percent copper

Edge: Reeded

Designer: Anthony de Francisci

TRADE DOLLARS

Diameter: 38.1 millimeters (1 1/2 inches)

Weight: 27.216 grams (0.960 ounce)

Composition: 90 percent silver, 10 percent copper

Edge: Reeded

Designer: William Barber

EISENHOWER DOLLARS

Diameter: 38.1 millimeters (1 1/2 inches)

Weight: 22.68 grams (0.800 ounce)

Composition: 75 percent copper, 25 percent nickel alloy bonded to a pure copper core

Edge: Reeded

Designer: Frank Gasparro

SUSAN B. ANTHONY DOLLARS

Diameter: 26.5 millimeters (about 1 1/20 inches)

Weight: 8.1 grams (0.286 ounce)

Composition: 75 percent copper, 25 percent nickel alloy bonded to a pure copper core

Edge: Reeded

Designer: Frank Gasparro

SACAGAWEA DOLLAR AND PRESIDENTIAL DOLLAR

Diameter: 26.5 millimeters (about 1 1/20 inches)

Weight: 8.1 grams (0.286 ounce)

Composition: 88.5 percent copper, 6 percent zinc, 3.5 percent manganese, 2 percent nickel (core: 50 percent copper; clad layers: 4 percent nickel, 77 percent copper, 12 percent zinc, 7 percent manganese)

Edge: Plain

Designers: Glenna Goodacre (obverse) and Thomas D. Rogers, Sr. (reverse)

GOLD DOLLARS

Diameter: 13 millimeters (about 1/2 inch) 1849–mid-1854, 14.86 millimeters (about 6/10 of an inch) mid-1854 and thereafter

Weight: 1.672 grams (0.059 ounce)

Composition: 90 percent gold, 10 percent copper and silver

Edge: Reeded

Designer: James B. Longacre

CAPPED BUST FACING RIGHT QUARTER EAGLES ($2.50 GOLD PIECE)

Diameter: About 20 millimeters (4/5 of an inch)

Weight: 4.374 grams (0.154 ounce)

Composition: 91.67 percent gold, 8.33 percent copper and silver

Edge: Reeded

Designer: Robert Scot

CAPPED BUST FACING LEFT QUARTER EAGLES

Diameter: About 20 millimeters (4/5 of an inch)

Weight: 4.374 grams (0.154 ounce)

Composition: 91.67 percent gold, 8.33 percent copper and silver

Edge: Reeded

Designer: John Reich

CAPPED HEAD QUARTER EAGLES

Diameter: 18.5 millimeters (about 3/4 of an inch) 1821–1827, 18.2 millimeters (about 7/10 of an inch) 1829–1834

Weight: 4.374 grams (0.154 ounce)

Composition: 91.67 percent gold, 8.33 percent copper and silver

Edge: Reeded

Designer: Robert Scot and John Reich

CLASSIC HEAD QUARTER EAGLES

Diameter: 18.2 millimeters (about 7/10 of an inch)

Weight: 4.18 grams (0.147 ounce)

Composition: 89.92 percent gold, 10.08 percent copper and silver 1834–1836; 90 percent gold, 10 percent copper and silver 1837–1839

Edge: Reeded

Designer: William Kneass

CORONET QUARTER EAGLES

Diameter: 18.2 millimeters (about 7/10 of an inch)

Weight: 4.18 grams (0.147 ounce)

Composition: 90 percent gold, 10 percent copper

Edge: Reeded

Designer: Christian Gobrecht

INDIAN HEAD QUARTER EAGLES

Diameter: 18 millimeters (about 7/10 of an inch)

Weight: 4.18 grams (0.147 ounce)

Composition: 90 percent gold, 10 percent copper

Edge: Reeded

Designer: Bela Lyon Pratt

THREE DOLLAR GOLD PIECES

Diameter: 20.5 millimeters (about 4/5 of an inch)

Weight: 5.015 grams (0.177 ounce)

Composition: 90 percent gold, 10 percent copper

Edge: Reeded

Designer: James B. Longacre

"STELLAS" (FOUR DOLLAR GOLD PIECES)

Diameter: 22 millimeters (about 7/8 of an inch)

Weight: 7 grams (0.247 ounce)

Composition: 85.71 percent gold, 4.29 percent silver, 10 percent copper

Edge: Reeded

Designers: Charles E. Barber and George T. Morgan

CAPPED BUST HALF EAGLES (FIVE DOLLAR GOLD PIECES)

Diameter: 25 millimeters (about 1 inch)

Weight: 8.748 grams (0.309 ounce)

Composition: 91.67 percent gold, 8.33 percent copper and silver

Edge: Reeded

Designer: Robert Scot

CAPPED DRAPED BUST FACING LEFT HALF EAGLES

Diameter: 25 millimeters (about 1 inch)

Weight: 8.748 grams (0.309 ounce)

Composition: 91.67 percent gold, 8.33 percent copper and silver

Edge: Reeded

Designer: John Reich

CAPPED HEAD HALF EAGLES

Diameter: 25 millimeters (about 1 inch) 1813–mid-1829, 23.8 millimeters (about 15/16 of an inch) mid-1829 and thereafter

Weight: 8.748 grams (0.309 ounce)

Composition: 91.67 percent gold, 8.33 percent copper and silver

Edge: Reeded

Designer: John Reich

CLASSIC HEAD HALF EAGLES

Diameter: 22.5 millimeters (about 7/8 of an inch)

Weight: 8.36 grams (0.295 ounce)

Composition: 89.92 percent gold, 10.08 percent copper

1834–1836, 90 percent gold, 10 percent copper and silver 1837–1838

Edge: Reeded

Designer: William Kneass

CORONET HALF EAGLES

Diameter: 22.5 millimeters (about 7/8 of an inch) 1839–mid-1840, 21.6 millimeters (about 17/20 of an inch) mid-1840 and thereafter

Weight: 8.36 grams (0.295 ounce)

Composition: 90 percent gold, 10 percent copper

Edge: Reeded

Designer: Christian Gobrecht

INDIAN HEAD HALF EAGLES

Diameter: 21.6 millimeters (about 17/20 of an inch)

Weight: 8.36 grams (0.295 ounce)

Composition: 90 percent gold, 10 percent copper

Edge: Reeded

Designer: Bela Lyon Pratt

CAPPED BUST EAGLES (TEN DOLLAR GOLD PIECES)

Diameter: 33 millimeters (about 1 15/16 inches)

Weight: 17.496 grams (0.617 ounce)

Composition: 91.67 percent gold, 8.33 percent copper and silver

Edge: Reeded

Designer: Robert Scot

CORONET EAGLES

Diameter: 27 millimeters (about 1 1/14 of an inch)

Weight: 16.718 grams (0.590 ounce)

Composition: 90 percent gold, 10 percent copper and silver 1838–mid-1873; 90 percent gold, 10 percent copper mid-1873 and thereafter

Edge: Reeded

Designer: Christian Gobrecht

INDIAN HEAD EAGLES

Diameter: 27 millimeters (about 1 1/14 of an inch)

Weight: 16.718 grams (0.590 ounce)

Composition: 90 percent gold, 10 percent copper

Edge: Starred (46 raised stars 1907–1911, 48 raised stars thereafter; each star represents one of the states in the Union, and two new states—New Mexico and Arizona—joined the Union in 1912)

Designer: Augustus Saint-Gaudens

LIBERTY HEAD DOUBLE EAGLES (TWENTY DOLLAR GOLD PIECES)

Diameter: 34.2 millimeters (about 1 1/3 inches)

Weight: 33.436 grams (1.80 ounces)

Composition: 90 percent gold, 10 percent copper and silver 1849–mid-1873; 90 percent gold, 10 percent copper mid-1873 and thereafter

Edge: Reeded

Designer: James B. Longacre

SAINT-GAUDENS DOUBLE EAGLES (TWENTY DOLLAR GOLD PIECES)

Diameter: 34.2 millimeters (about 1 1/3 inches)

Weight: 33.436 grams (1.80 ounces)

Composition: 90 percent gold, 10 percent copper

Edge: Lettered E PLURIBUS UNUM, with stars dividing the words

Designer: Augustus Saint-Gaudens

APPENDIX B:

Notable Coin-related Legislation

THE COINAGE ACT OF 1792

The Coinage Act of 1792 was the original basis for the coinage of the new United States and served as the basis of coinage standards for decades. Subsequent coinage acts slowly changed the original standards. The Coinage Act of 1849 added new denominations of gold coins. In 1864, the coinage act of that year added in the inscription "In God We Trust" to all U.S. coins. The 1873 coinage act demonetized silver and made the Mint part of the Treasury. The Coinage Act of 1965 removed silver from American pocket change.

An examination of the 1792 act is important in understanding the delineation between money backed by metals and the fiat currencies of today.

THE COINAGE ACT OF 1792

United States Statutes at Large, 2nd Cong., Sess. I., pp. 246–251
April 2, 1792

An Act Establishing a Mint, and regulating the Coins of the United States.

Section 1. Be it enacted by the Senate and House of Representatives of the United States of America in Congress assembled, and it is hereby enacted and declared, That a mint for the purpose of a national coinage be, and the same is established; to be situate and carried on at the seat of the government of the United States, for the time being: And that for the well conducting of the business of the said mint, there shall be the following officers and persons, namely,—a Director, an Assayer, a Chief Coiner, an Engraver, a Treasurer.

Section 2. And be it further enacted, That the Director of the mint shall employ as many clerks, workmen and servants, as he shall from time to time find necessary, subject to the approbation of the President of the United States.

Section 3. And be it further enacted, That the respective functions and duties of the officers above mentioned shall be as follow: The Director of the mint shall have the chief management of the business thereof, and shall superintend all other officers and persons who shall be employed therein. The Assayer shall receive and give receipts for all metals which may lawfully be brought to the mint to be coined; shall assay all such of them as may require it, and shall deliver them to the Chief Coiner to be coined. The Chief Coiner shall cause to be coined all metals which shall be received by him for that purpose, according to such regulations as shall be prescribed by this or any future law. The Engraver shall sink and prepare the necessary dies for such coinage, with the proper devices and inscriptions, but it shall be lawful for the functions and duties of Chief Coiner and Engraver to be performed by one person. The Treasurer shall receive from the Chief Coiner all the coins which shall have been struck, and shall pay or deliver them to the persons respectively to whom the same ought to be paid or delivered: he shall moreover receive and safely keep all monies which shall be for the use, maintenance and support of the mint, and shall disburse the same upon warrants signed by the Director.

Section 4. And be it further enacted, That every officer and clerk of the said mint shall, before he enters upon the execution of his office, take an oath or affirmation before some judge of the United States faithfully and diligently to perform the duties thereof.

Section 5. And be it further enacted, That the said assayer, chief coiner and treasurer, previously to entering upon the execution of their respective offices, shall each become bound to the United States of America, with one or more sureties to the satisfaction of the Secretary of the Treasury, in the sum of ten thousand dollars, with condition for the faithful and diligent performance of the duties of his office.

Section 6. And be it further enacted, That there shall be allowed and paid as compensations for their respective services—To the said director, a yearly salary of two thousand dollars, to the said assayer, a yearly salary of one thousand five hundred dollars, to the said chief coiner, a yearly salary of one thousand five hundred dollars, to the said engraver, a yearly salary of one thousand two hundred dollars, to the said treasurer, a yearly salary of one thousand two hundred dollars, to each clerk who may be employed, a yearly salary not exceeding five hundred dollars, and to the several subordinate workmen and servants, such wages and allowances as are customary and reasonable, according to their respective stations and occupations.

Section 7. And be it further enacted, That the accounts of the officers and persons employed in and about the said mint and for services performed in relation thereto, and all other accounts concerning the business and administration thereof, shall be adjusted and settled in the treasury department of the United States, and a quarter yearly account of the receipts and disbursements of the said mint shall be rendered at the said treasury for settlement according to such forms and regulations as shall have been prescribed by that department; and that once in each year a report of the transactions of the said mint, accompanied by an abstract of the settlements which shall have been from time to time made, duly certified by the comptroller of the treasury, shall be laid before Congress for their information.

Section 8. And be it further enacted, That in addition to the authority vested in the President of the United States by a resolution of the last session, touching the engaging of artists and the procuring of apparatus for the said mint, the President be authorized, and he is hereby authorized to cause to be provided and put in proper condition such buildings, and in such manner as shall appear to him requisite for the purpose of carrying on the business of the said mint; and that as well the expenses which shall have been incurred pursuant to the said resolution as those which may be incurred in providing and preparing the said buildings, and all other expenses which may hereafter accrue for the maintenance and support of the said mint, and in carrying on the business thereof, over and above the sums which may be received by reason of the rate per centum for coinage herein after mentioned, shall be defrayed from the treasury of the United States, out of any monies which from time to time shall be therein, not otherwise appropriated.

Section 9. And be it further enacted, That there shall be from time to time struck and coined at the said mint, coins of gold, silver, and copper, of the following denominations, values and descriptions, viz. Eagles—each to be of the value of ten dollars or units, and to contain two hundred and forty-seven grains and four eighths of a grain of pure, or two hundred and seventy grains of standard gold. Half Eagles—each to be of the value of five dollars, and to contain one hundred and twenty-three grains and six eighths of a grain of pure, or one hundred and thirty-five grains of standard gold. Quarter Eagles—each to be of the value of two dollars and a half dollar, and to contain sixty-one grains and seven eighths of a grain of pure, or sixty-seven grains and four eighths of a grain of standard gold. Dollars or Units—each to be of the value of a Spanish milled dollar as the same is now current, and to contain three hundred and seventy-one grains and four sixteenth parts of a grain of pure, or four hundred and sixteen grains of standard silver. Half Dollars—each to be of half the value of the dollar or unit, and to contain one hundred and eighty-five grains and ten sixteenth parts of a grain of pure, or two hundred and eight grains of standard silver. Quarter Dollars—each to be of one fourth the value of the dollar or unit, and to contain ninety-two grains and thirteen sixteenth parts of a grain of pure, or one hundred and four grains of standard silver. Dismes*—each to be of the value of one tenth of a dollar or unit, and to contain thirty-seven grains and

---

* A disme (from the French, meaning "one-tenth") was the original term for a dime. Disme and half-disme coins were minted only in 1792; only a few hundred exist today.

two sixteenth parts of a grain of pure, or forty-one grains and three fifth parts of a grain of standard silver. Half Dismes—each to be of the value of one twentieth of a dollar, and to contain eighteen grains and nine sixteenth parts of a grain of pure, or twenty grains and four fifth parts of a grain of standard silver. Cents—each to be of the value of the one hundredth part of a dollar, and to contain eleven penny-weights of copper. Half Cents—each to be of the value of half a cent, and to contain five penny-weights and half a penny-weight of copper.

Section 10. And be it further enacted, That, upon the said coins respectively, there shall be the following devices and legends, namely: Upon one side of each of the said coins there shall be an impression emblematic of liberty, with an inscription of the word Liberty, and the year of the coinage; and upon the reverse of each of the gold and silver coins there shall be the figure or representation of an eagle, with this inscription, "United States of America" and upon the reverse of each of the copper coins, there shall be an inscription which shall express the denomination of the piece, namely, cent or half cent, as the case may require.

Section 11. And be it further enacted, That the proportional value of gold to silver in all coins which shall by law be current as money within the United States, shall be as fifteen to one, according to quantity in weight, of pure gold or pure silver; that is to say, every fifteen pounds weight of pure silver shall be of equal value in all payments, with one pound weight of pure gold, and so in proportion as to any greater or less quantities of the respective metals.

Section 12. And be if further enacted, That the standard for all gold coins of the United States shall be eleven parts fine to one part alloy; and accordingly that eleven parts in twelve of the entire weight of each of the said coins shall consist of pure gold, and the remaining one twelfth part of alloy; and the said alloy shall be composed of silver and copper, in such proportions not exceeding one half silver as shall be found convenient; to be regulated by the director of the mint, for the time being, with the approbation of the President of the United States, until further provision shall be made by law. And to the end that the necessary information may be had in order to the making of such further provision, it shall be the duty of the director of the mint, at the expiration of a year after commencing the operations of the said mint, to report to Congress the practice thereof during the said year, touching the composition of the alloy of the said gold coins, the reasons for such practice, and the experiments and observations which shall have been made concerning the effects of different proportions of silver and copper in the said alloy.

Section 13. And be it further enacted, That the standard for all silver coins of the United States, shall be one thousand four hundred and eighty-five parts fine to one hundred and seventy-nine parts alloy; and accordingly that one thousand four hundred and eighty-five parts in one thousand six hundred and sixty-four parts of the entire weight of each of the said coins shall consist of pure silver, and the remaining one hundred and seventy-nine parts of alloy; which alloy shall be wholly of copper.

Section 14. And be it further enacted, That it shall be lawful for any person or persons to bring to the said mint gold and silver bullion, in order to their being coined; and that the bullion so brought shall be there assayed and coined as speedily as may be after the receipt thereof, and that free of expense of the person or persons by whom the same shall have been brought. And as soon as the said bullion shall have been coined, the person or persons by whom the same shall have been delivered, shall upon demand receive in lieu thereof coins of the same species of bullion which shall have been so delivered, weight for weight, of the pure gold or pure silver therein contained: Provided nevertheless, That it shall be at the mutual option of the party or parties bringing such bullion, and of the director of the said mint, to make an immediate exchange of coins for standard bullion, with a deduction of one half per cent from the weight of the pure gold, or pure silver contained in the said bullion, as an indemnification to the mint for the time which will necessarily be required for coining the said bullion, and for the advance which have been so made in coins. And it shall be the duty of the Secretary of the Treasury to furnish the said mint from time to time whenever the state of the treasury will admit thereof, with such sums as may be necessary for effecting the said exchanges, to be replaced as speedily as may be out of the coins which shall have been made of the bullion for which the monies so furnished shall have been exchanged; and the said deduction of one half per cent shall constitute a fund towards defraying the expenses of the said mint.

Section 15. And be it further enacted, That the bullion which shall be brought as aforesaid to the mint to be coined, shall be coined, and the equivalent thereof in coins rendered, if demanded, in the order in which the said bullion shall have been brought or delivered, giving priority according to priority of delivery only, and without preference to any person or persons; and if any preference shall be given contrary to the direction aforesaid, the officer by whom such undue preference shall be given, shall in each case forfeit and pay one thousand dollars, to be recovered with costs of suit. And to the end that it may be known if such preference shall at any time be given, the assayer or officer to whom the said bullion shall be delivered to be coined, shall give to the person or persons bringing the same, a memorandum in writing under his hand, denoting the weight, fineness and value thereof, together with the day and order of its delivery into the mint.

Section 16. And be it further enacted, That all the gold and silver coins which shall have been struck at, and issued from the said mint, shall be a lawful tender in all payments whatsoever, those of full weight according to the respective values herein before declared, and those of less than full weight of values proportional to their respective weights.

Section 17. And be it further enacted, That it shall be the duty of the respective officers of the said mint, carefully and faithfully to use their best endeavors that all the gold and silver coins which shall be struck at the said mint shall be, as nearly as may be, conformable to the several standards and weights aforesaid, and that the copper whereof the cents and half cents aforesaid may be composed, shall be of good quality.

Section 18. And the better to secure a due conformity of the said gold and silver coins to their respective standards. Be it further enacted, That from every separate mass of standard gold or silver, which shall be made into coins at the said mint, there shall be taken, set apart by the treasurer and reserved in his custody a certain number of pieces, not less than three, and that once in every year the pieces so set apart and reserved, shall be assayed under the inspection of the Chief Justice of the United States, the Secretary and Comptroller of the Treasury, the Secretary for the department of State, and the Attorney General of the United States (who are hereby required to attend for that purpose at the said mint, on the last Monday in July in each year), or under the inspection of any three of them, in such manner as they or a majority of them shall direct, and in the presence of the director, assayer and chief coiner of the said mint; and if it shall be found that the gold and silver so assayed, shall not be inferior to their respective standards herein before declared more than one part in one hundred and forty-four parts, the officer or officers of the said mint whom it may concern shall be held excusable; but if any greater inferiority shall appear, it shall be certified to the President of the United States, and the said officer or officers shall be deemed disqualified to hold their respective offices.

Section 19. And be it further enacted, That if any of the gold or silver coins which shall be struck or coined at the said mint shall be debased or made worse as to the proportion of fine gold or fine silver therein contained, or shall be of less weight or value than the same ought to be pursuant to the directions of this act, through the default or with the connivance of any of the officers or persons who shall be employed at the said mint, for the purpose of profit or gain, or otherwise with a fraudulent intent, and if any of the said officers or persons shall embezzle any of the metals which shall at any time be committed to their charge for the purpose of being coined, or any of the coins which shall be struck or coined at the said mint, every such officer or person who shall commit any or either of the said offences, shall be deemed guilty of felony, and shall suffer death.

Section 20. And be it further enacted, That the money of account of the United States shall be expressed in dollars or units, dismes or tenth, cents or hundredths, and miles or thousandths, a disme being the tenth part of a dollar, a cent the hundredth part of a dollar, a mile the thousandth part of a dollar, and that all accounts in the public offices and all proceedings in the courts of the United States shall be kept and had in conformity to this regulation.

Approved, April 2, 1792.

AN EXECUTIVE ORDER CONFISCATING PRIVATELY HELD GOLD

In 1933, shortly after he took office, President Franklin D. Roosevelt confiscated, or forbade the hoard of gold coin, bullion, and certificates; some consider it a day of infamy. The Mint would not offer gold bullion for decades to come.

PRESIDENTIAL EXECUTIVE ORDER 6102

Forbidding the Hoarding of Gold Coin, Gold Bullion and Gold Certificates Issued April 5, 1933

By virtue of the authority vested in me by Section 5(b) of the Act of October 6, 1917, as amended by Section 2 of the Act of March 9, 1933, entitled "An Act to provide relief in the existing national emergency in banking, and for other purposes," in which amendatory Act Congress declared that a serious emergency exists, I, Franklin D. Roosevelt, President of the United States of America, do declare that said national emergency still continues to exist and pursuant to said section to do hereby prohibit the hoarding gold coin, gold bullion, and gold certificates within the continental United States by individuals, partnerships, associations and corporations and hereby prescribe the following regulations for carrying out the purposes of the order:

Section 1. For the purpose of this regulation, the term "hoarding" means the withdrawal and withholding of gold coin, gold bullion, and gold certificates from the recognized and customary channels of trade. The term "person" means any individual, partnership, association or corporation.

Section 2. All persons are hereby required to deliver on or before May 1, 1933, to a Federal Reserve bank or a branch or agency thereof or to any member bank of the Federal Reserve System all gold coin, gold bullion, and gold certificates now owned by them or coming into their ownership on or before April 28, 1933, except the following:

(A) Such amount of gold as may be required for legitimate and customary use in industry, profession or art within a reasonable time, including gold prior to refining and stocks of gold in reasonable amounts for the usual trade requirements of owners mining and refining such gold.

(B) Gold coin and gold certificates in an amount not exceeding in the aggregate $100.00 belonging to any one person; and gold coins having recognized special value to collectors of rare and unusual coins.

(C) Gold coin and bullion earmarked or held in trust for a recognized foreign government or foreign central bank or the Bank for International Settlements.

(D) Gold coin and bullion licensed for the other proper transactions (not involving hoarding) including gold coin and gold bullion imported for the re-export or held pending action on applications for export license.

Section 3. Until otherwise ordered any person becoming the owner of any gold coin, gold bullion, and gold certificates after April 28, 1933, shall within three days after receipt thereof, deliver the same in the manner prescribed in Section 2; unless such gold coin, gold bullion, and gold certificates are held for any of the purposes specified in paragraphs (a), (b), or (c) of Section 2; or unless such gold coin, gold bullion is held for purposes specified in paragraph (d) of Section 2 and the person holding it is, with respect to such gold coin or bullion, a licensee or applicant for license pending action thereon.

Section 4. Upon receipt of gold coin, gold bullion, or gold certificates delivered to it in accordance with Section 2 or 3, the Federal reserve bank or member bank will pay thereof an equivalent amount of any other form of coin or currency coined or issued under the laws of the United States.

Section 5. Member banks shall deliver all gold coin, gold bullion, and gold certificates owned or received by them (other than as exempted under the provisions of Section 2) to the Federal reserve banks of their respective districts and receive credit or payment thereof.

Section 6. The Secretary of the Treasury, out of the sum made available to the President by Section 501 of the Act of March 9, 1933, will in all proper cases pay the reasonable costs of transportation of gold coin, gold bullion, and gold certificates delivered to a member bank or Federal reserve bank in accordance with Sections 2, 3, or 5 hereof, including the cost of insurance, protection, and such other incidental costs as may be necessary, upon production of satisfactory evidence of such costs. Voucher forms for this purpose may be procured from Federal reserve banks.

Section 7. In cases where the delivery of gold coin, gold bullion, or gold certificates by the owners thereof within the time set forth above will involve extraordinary hardship or difficulty, the Secretary of the Treasury may, in his discretion, extend the time within which such delivery must be made. Applications for such extensions must be made in writing under oath; addressed to the Secretary of the Treasury and filed with a Federal reserve bank. Each application must state the date to which the extension is desired, the amount and location of the gold coin, gold bullion, and gold certificates in respect of which such application is made and the facts showing extension to be necessary to avoid extraordinary hardship or difficulty.

Section 8. The Secretary of the Treasury is hereby authorized and empowered to issue such further regulations as he may deem necessary to carry the purposes of this order and to issue licenses thereunder, through such officers or agencies as he may designate, including licenses permitting the Federal reserve banks and member banks of the Federal Reserve System, in return for an equivalent amount of other coin, currency or credit, to deliver, earmark or hold in trust gold coin or bullion to or for persons showing the need for same for any of the purposes specified in paragraphs (a), (c), and (d) of Section 2 of these regulations.

Section 9. Whoever willfully violates any provision of this Executive Order or these regulation or of any rule, regulation or license issued thereunder may be fined not more than $10,000, or, if a natural person may be imprisoned for not more than ten years or both; and any officer, director, or agent of any corporation who knowingly participates in any such violation may be punished by a like fine, imprisonment, or both.

This order and these regulations may be modified or revoked at any time.

Franklin D. Roosevelt
President of the United States of America
April 5, 1933

THE GOLD BULLION COIN ACT OF 1985

Following Roosevelt's Presidential Order 6102, more than five decades would pass before the return of gold bullion sales by the U.S. Mint. America was off the gold standard, and hoarding no longer seen as a danger to the money supply. It was time for the federal government to address the people's desire to bring gold bullion sales back.

AN ACT

to authorize the minting of gold bullion coins.

Be it in enacted by the Senate and House of Representatives of the United States of America in Congress assembled,

Short Title

Section 1. This Act may be cited as the "**Gold Bullion Coin Act of 1985.**"

Minting Gold Bullion Coins

Sec. 2. (A) Section 5112(a) of the title 31, United States Code, is amended by adding at the end thereof the following new paragraphs:

"(7) A fifty dollar gold coin that is 32.7 millimeters in diameter, weighs 33.931 grams, and contains one troy ounce of fine gold.

"(8) A twenty-five dollar gold coin that is 27.0 millimeters in diameter, weighs 16.996 grams, and contains one-half troy ounce of fine gold.

"(9) A ten dollar gold coin that is 22.0 millimeters in diameter, weighs 8.483 grams, and contains one-fourth troy ounce of fine gold.

"(10) A five dollar gold coin that is 16.5 millimeters in diameter, weighs 3.393 grams, and contains one-tenth troy ounce of fine gold."

(B) Section 5112 of title 31, United States Code, is amended by adding at the end thereof the following new subsection:

"(1) Notwithstanding section 5111 (a)(1) of this title, the Secretary shall mint and issue the gold coins described in paragraphs (7), (8), (9), and (10) of subsection (a) of this section, in quantities sufficient to meet public demand, and such gold coins shall

"(a) have a design determined by the Secretary, except that the fifty dollar gold coin shall have—"(i) on the obverse side, a design symbolic of Liberty; and "(ii) on the reverse side, a design representing a FAMILY OF EAGLES, with the male carrying an olive branch and flying above a nest containing a female eagle and hatchlings;

"(b) have inscriptions of the denomination, the weight of the fine gold content, the year of minting or issuance, and the words 'Liberty', 'In God We Trust,' 'United States of America,' and 'E Pluribus Unum,' and

"(c) have reeded edges.

"(2)(a) The Secretary shall sell the coins minted under this subsection to the public at a price equal to the market value of the bullion at the time of sale, plus the cost of minting, marketing, and distributing such coins (including labor, materials, dies, use of machinery, and promotional and overhead expenses).

"(b) The Secretary shall make bulk sales of the coins minted under this subsection at a reasonable discount.

"(3) For purposes of section 5132(a)(1) of this title, all coins minted under this subsection shall be considered to be numismatic items."

(c) Section 5116(a) of title 31, United States Code, is amended by adding at the end thereof the following:

"(4) The Secretary shall acquire gold for the coins issued under section 5112(i) of this title by purchase of gold mined from natural deposits in the United States, or in a territory or possession of the United States, within one year after the month in which the ore from which it is derived was mined. The Secretary shall pay not more than the average world price for the gold. In the absence of available supplies of such gold at the average world price, the Secretary may use gold from reserves held by the United States to mint the coins issued under section 5112(i) of this title. The Secretary shall issue such regulations as may be necessary to carry out this paragraph."

(D) Section 5118(b) of title 31, United States Code, is amended—

(1) in the first sentence, by striking out "or deliver"; and

(2) in the second sentence, by inserting "(other than gold and silver coins)" before "that may be lawfully held."

(E) The third sentence of section 5132(a)(1) of title 31, United States Code, is amended by striking out "minted under section 5112(a) of this title" and inserting in lieu thereof "minted under paragraphs (1) through (6) of section 5112(a) of this title."

(F) Notwithstanding any other provision of law, an amount equal to the amount by which the proceeds from the sale of the coins issued under section 5112(i) of title 31, United States Code, exceed the sum of—

(1) the cost of minting, marketing, and distributing such coins, and

(2) the value of gold certificates (not exceeding forty-two and two-ninths dollars a fine troy ounce) retired from the use of gold contained in such coins, shall be deposited in the general fund of the Treasury and shall be used for the sole purpose of reducing the national debt.

(G) The Secretary shall take all actions necessary to ensure that the issuance of the coins minted under Section 5112(i) of title 31, United States Code, shall result in no net cost to the United States Government.

PUBLIC LAW 99–185—DEC. 17, 1985 99 STAT. 1179

effective date

Sec 3. This Act shall take effect on October 1, 1985, except that no coins may be issued or sold under section 5112(i) of title 31, United States Code, before October 1, 1986.

APPENDIX C:

Glossary

Many definitions are adapted, with permission, from *The Coin Collector's Survival Manual*, by Scott Travers, and from the Numismatic Guaranty Corporation (NGC).

About Uncirculated: The grades AU-50, AU-53, AU-55, and AU-58. A coin that on first glance appears Uncirculated but upon closer inspection has slight friction or rub.

abrasion: An acquired mark or nick that mars a coin's surface and lowers its visual appeal.

abrasive: The category of chemicals or substances which, if used on coins, will abrade or scrape away the top layer of metal.

accumulation: A hoard or group of coins being held at a common location.

Ag: The chemical symbol for silver.

album: A holder used by collectors to store coins of a series. A useful way to assess progress in completing a collection.

alloy: A solid solution made by melting two or more metals together. Most U.S. coins are made of alloys, rather than a single metal.

altered: A (usually) genuine but common coin that has been tampered with to make it resemble a rare coin.

ANA: American Numismatic Association, world's largest coin collector organization.

appraisal: A professional opinion offered by a dealer. Appraisals are rarely objective because dealers like to buy coins for less than they are worth.

arbitrage: A strategy involving the simultaneous purchase and sale of identical or equivalent commodity futures contracts or other instruments across two or more markets in order to benefit from a discrepancy in their price relationship.

Ask: The "Ask" column of the *Coin Dealer Newsletter*. List of coin prices that wholesale dealers are asking for particular coins.

assay: The testing of an ore sample to determine its precious-metal value.

attribution: The description and background information a coin is given in a dealer's retail catalog, auction catalog, etc. Does not refer to a grade.

Au: The chemical symbol for gold.

authentication: The determination of a coin's genuineness.

backwardation: A commodities future structure in which prices for future deliveries are lower than the spot price—generally a sign of unusual near-term demand.

bag mark: A mark on a coin's surface that has been acquired through contact with another coin or coins banging around inside a Mint-sewn bag.

base metal: A nonprecious metal, such as copper, nickel, or zinc.

bear: One who expects a decline in prices. The opposite of a bull.

bear market: A market in which the primary trend is down, often more than 20 percent below its recent peak. The opposite of a bull market.

Bid: The "Bid" column of the *Coin Dealer Newsletter*. Refers to wholesale prices dealers are offering to pay for certain coins.

blank: A disc (usually round) on which a coin is to be struck.

BN: Abbreviation for brown copper coins.

body bag: A coin deemed to be ungradable because of tampering is sent back to a person in a plastic pouch known as a "body bag."

bourse: A popular term for the sales floor of a coin show.

branch mint: A coin-producing U.S. Mint facility other than the main mint in Philadelphia.

brass: An alloy of copper and zinc.

brilliant: A term used to describe the bright, untoned surfaces of certain U.S. coins, especially proofs.

broadstruck: A minting error resulting from a coin being struck without a collar that causes the surface features of a coin to spread out.

bronze: An alloy of copper and tin.

BU coin: A brilliant uncirculated coin; often grades at MS-65 or higher.

bull: One who expects a rise in prices. The opposite of a bear.

bullion: Refined precious metal in non-coin form.

bull market: A market in which the primary trend is up, often 20 percent and rising from its recent low.

business strike: A coin manufactured by the Mint for everyday use.

cabinet friction: A specific type of wear on a coin that has circulated slightly. The term originated in dealers' catalogs years ago when coins were stored in elaborate cabinets with velvet trays.

The coins slid about on these trays and developed "cabinet friction" on their highest points.

cameo: Usually denotes a contrast between frosted fields and reflective devices.

carbon flecks/carbon spots: Usually spots that are not really carbon, but dense areas of toning on a coin's surface. These spots, attributed to mishandling, are darkened areas resulting from contact with saliva.

cartwheel: A term for a silver dollar, suggesting its large size in relation to other coins.

cataloger: The individual who assigns a grade to a coin or coins in a dealer's catalog (e.g., retail or auction).

CDN: Shorthand for the *Coin Dealer Newsletter*, a widely used weekly price guide often called the "Greysheet."

central bank: The entity responsible for establishing a nation's monetary policy and controlling the money supply and interest rates.

CFTC: Commodity Futures Trading Commission; an independent agency with the mandate to regulate commodity futures and option markets in the United States.

choice: An adjective used to describe a Mint State coin that is better than ordinary but less than gem.

circulated: A term for a coin that has been passed from hand to hand and shows evidence of wear.

clad: A type of coin made by the U.S. Mint since 1965 that consists of two outer layers of copper-nickel alloy bonded to a core of pure copper.

clashed die: A die that has been damaged after being struck by another die which then imparts damage marks to coins that are struck with the damaged die.

collar: A retaining ring that imparts a coin's edge, whether plain or reeded.

COMEX: A U.S. exchange market for gold, silver, copper, palladium, and aluminum futures contracts, operated by Commodity Exchange, Inc., a subsidiary of New York Mercantile Exchange, Inc., of the CME Group.

commemorative coins: Special coins issued to mark an important event or honor a person or organization. Due to lower populations, the coins are generally not spent.

common-date coins: Coins that were struck in large quantities and are easy to procure and generally inexpensive compared to their key-date counterparts.

condition census: A designation awarded to a coin in the finest existing condition of a given issue. Does not refer to the finest condition ever known or the finest condition possible.

consignor: Someone whose coins are sold by an auction company.

contact marks: Small nicks imparted by contact with other coins.

Contango market: A futures market in which prices are higher in the succeeding delivery months than in the nearest delivery month. The opposite of backwardation.

Coronet Head: A nineteenth-century coin on which Lady Liberty wears a coronet (lesser crown).

correction: A decline in prices following a rise in a market; the decline is usually about 10 percent in size.

corrosion: Rust or similar unsightly damage on the surface of a coin, usually caused by a chemical reaction.

counterfeit: A non-genuine coin, whether made to circulate as money or to deceive collectors.

crack-out: To crack a coin out of a plastic holder in order to resubmit it to a grading service in hopes of receiving a higher, more valuable grade.

currency: Circulating money, used numismatically to denote a non-proof coin.

cycle: The historical boom-and-bust price performance tendency of the coin market.

denarius: A silver ancient Roman coin that was eventually devalued to contain very little silver.

denomination: The face value of a coin, such as cent, nickel, or dime.

denticles: The toothlike projections seen on the borders of older U.S. coins.

detraction: An imperfection, either Mint-made or acquired, which detracts from a coin's grade or value or both.

devices: The raised parts on a coin, such as the lettering, portrait, and stars.

die: A cylindrical steel shaft engraved with a coin's design, used to strike or stamp out coins (two dies are required for each coin).

DMPL: Shorthand for Deep Mirror Prooflike, a term applied to coins—especially silver dollars—with unusually brilliant, reflective surfaces.

doubled-die: Term applied to coins with doubling of the letters and date resulting from the die itself having been struck twice in misaligned positions.

Double Eagle: A United States twenty dollar gold coin, issued from 1849 to 1933.

double-struck: A condition that results when a coin is not ejected from the dies and is struck a second time. Such a coin is said to be double-struck. Triple-struck coins and other multiple strikings also are known. Proofs are usually double-struck on purpose in order to sharpen their details; this is sometimes visible only under magnification.

Eagle: A U.S. ten dollar gold coin, issued from 1795 to 1933.

edge: A coin's side; the part you touch when you hold a coin properly. This is not to be confused with obverse (front) or reverse (back).

encapsulated coin: A coin that has been sealed inside a plastic holder.

estimate: A dealer's written approximation in his or her auction catalog of what a coin is worth and what it might sell for at that auction.

exhibit: A display of coins with educational information shown at a coin show and competing for a prize.

eye appeal: A subjective (and thus controversial) ingredient of coin grading that measures a coin's general attractiveness, based on color or quality of toning and strike.

face value: The amount of money a coin represents as a medium of exchange. For example, the face value of a nickel is five cents.

FB: Abbreviation for Full Split Bands designation, most notably on Mercury dimes.

FBL: Abbreviation for Full Bell Lines designation, most notably on Franklin half dollars.

field: The (usually flat) part of the coin that serves as background to the devices.

fineness: The percentage or decimal proportion of precious metal in a coin. For example: An American Double Gold Eagle is .9167 fine, meaning it is made up of 91.67 percent gold.

flip: A pliable, two-pocket coin holder that folds over. The coin is inserted in one pocket; a written description of the coin is inserted in the other pocket.

frosted: Describes a textured, rather than smooth or glassy, surface of a coin.

FT: Abbreviation for Full Torch designation on Roosevelt dimes.

gem: A Mint State coin of unusually high quality.

gold bug: A person who is a gold bull and expects the price of gold to advance.

gold standard: The backing of a currency by gold held by a sovereign government.

grade: The numerical value assigned to a coin's condition on a scale of 1 to 70.

grading service: A service that assigns a grade to a coin on a scale of 1 to 70.

Greysheet: The nickname for the *Coin Dealer Newsletter* (CDN), a weekly publication essential for successful coin transactions, and the *CDN Monthly Supplement,* the CDN's monthly publication. These are the most relied-upon guides for accurate prices.

hairlines: A patch or patches of light, almost unnoticeable scratches, especially on proof coins. Usually caused by cleaning.

half-cent: A U.S. copper coin of that value, issued from 1793 to 1857.

Half Eagle: A U.S. five dollar gold coin, issued from 1795 to 1929.

high relief: A term for a coin on which the design elements stand out above the surface more than usual. High-relief coins typically possess sharp detail, but their high points are exposed and abnormally subject to wear.

hoard: A group of coins held for either numismatic or monetary reasons.

hub: A steel cylinder bearing one side of a coin's design and used to produce dies.

impaired proof: A proof that has been mishandled, so that its grade is equivalent to that of a circulated business-strike coin.

insert: A sturdy piece of paper bearing a description of a coin that is inserted into one pocket of a flip-type coin holder.

intrinsic value: The value of a coin's metal, irrespective of its face or collector value.

investment grade coins: Coins with the greatest potential to appreciate in value, usually high graded and rare.

Judd: J. Hewitt Judd, M.D., author of *United States Pattern, Experimental and Trial Pieces,* a popular reference work written about pattern coins (issued most recently in an edition edited by Q. David Bowers with pricing by Robert L. Hughes). Each pattern is given a "Judd number." These numbers are referred to almost anytime a pattern is offered for sale. "Judd" refers to both the author and the book.

junk dealer: A dealer who sells inexpensive and relatively common circulated coins, as well as rolls of uncirculated recent-issue coins.

key date coins: Highly sought after coins that are scarce and generally much more expensive that common date coins.

Kointain: A trademark and popular name for a transparent, curvilinear triacetate coin capsule that fits snugly around the coin and is used to protect it.

Krugerrand: A South African gold coin, minted since 1967.

LBMA: The London Bullion Market Association. A trade association that acts as the coordinator for activities conducted on behalf of its members and other participants in the London bullion market.

legal tender: A coin declared by a government to be acceptable in the payment of all debts.

legend: An inscription on a coin.

lettered edge: A term used to describe an edge inscribed with letters and/or numbers.

luster: The full sheen or reflected light created by a coin, not to be confused with a shiny coin that may reflect light because it has been unnaturally polished.

market-maker: A dealer who makes offers to buy certified coins sight-unseen.

matte proof: A proof produced by a process that imparts dull, granular surfaces, sometimes said to have a "sandblast" appearance.

melt value: The value of a coin's raw material components.

minor coin: A base-metal coin of small value, such as a cent or nickel.

mintage: The number of examples of a given coin produced with the same date at a given mint.

mint error: A coin with a mistake that occurred during its manufacture. Some collectors collect only mint errors.

mint mark: The letter or letters on a coin indicating where it was minted. (Abbreviations for U.S. coins: P = Philadelphia; O = New Orleans; CC = Carson City; S = San Francisco; D = Denver or (on pre-1862 gold coins) Dahlonega; W = West Point; C = Charlotte.)

Mint State: The condition of a coin that has not circulated. Mint State coins should not exhibit wear. The terms Mint State and uncirculated are synonymous.

mirror: The brilliant surface of a coin, typically the fields of a proof- or prooflike coin.

motto: An inscription on a coin, such as LIBERTY, IN GOD WE TRUST, and E PLURIBUS UNUM.

MS: Abbreviation for Mint State.

mutilated: An adjective describing a coin that has been damaged or defaced in an obvious way.

national show: A coin convention attended by dealers from throughout the country.

NCI-certified: Authenticated and graded by the Numismatic Certification Institute, a division of Heritage Capital Corporation, a coin dealership. The coin should be accompanied by a photo-certificate. NCI no longer actively grades, but its 1985 standard is regarded as a coin-grading benchmark.

NGC-certified: Authenticated and graded by the Numismatic Guaranty Corporation of America. The coin should be encapsulated in a tamper-resistant holder.

nonabrasive: The category of chemicals or substances that, if applied to coins, will not remove the top layer of metal. Nonabrasives are usually not harmful to coins.

numismatics: The studying and collecting of coins.

obverse: The front or "heads" side of a coin.

off-center: A term for a coin struck on a planchet improperly aligned with the dies, so that the design elements aren't centered.

ounce: For the purposes of precious metals, this refers to a troy ounce, based on the troy weight system, in which a pound equals twelve ounces. (In contrast, in the avoirdupois weight system—used for goods other than precious metals, gems, and drugs in the U.S. and Great Britain—a pound equals sixteen ounces.) A troy ounce is equal to 1.0971428 avoirdupois ounces, and has a minimum fineness of 0.999.

overdate: A coin variety in which one date is impressed over another.

overgrading: Placing a coin in a higher grade than it deserves.

overpaying: Paying more money for a coin than the coin is worth.

overtones: Traces of toning colors on a coin that is toned one primary color.

patina: The brownish color that forms on the top layer of metal on copper coins.

pattern coin: A coin struck by the Mint to see how an experimental design would look if made into a coin.

PCGS-certified: Authenticated and graded by the Professional Coin Grading Service. The coin should be encapsulated in a tamper-resistant holder.

periphery: The outermost area of a coin's obverse or reverse.

PF: Abbreviation for proof; it's used with a numerical figure to grade a proof coin.

Photograde: A grading guide to circulated coins, by James F. Ruddy, that includes photographs of coins. (Full title: *Photograde: Official Photographic Grading Guide for United States Coins.*)

PL: Abbreviation for prooflike, a term applied to a business-strike coin whose brilliant surfaces resemble those of a proof.

plain edge: A term used when the side of a coin is smooth, not reeded or lettered.

planchet: A blank disc ready to receive impressions from two dies and become a coin.

polyvinyl chloride (PVC): A plastic found in many popular coin holders. Destructive to valuable uncirculated coins.

premium: The amount of money a coin is worth above its face value. This value is set in the rare-coin marketplace.

premium quality (PQ): Refers to a coin of one grade which nearly qualifies to be assigned the next-highest grade.

preservation: Refers to how well a coin has been kept since it was struck. Careful steps have to be taken by the collector to make sure that coins are meticulously stored and remain well preserved.

press: A compression machine in which dies come together to stamp a coin.

prices realized: The list of actual prices for which coins were sold in auction; usually available from the auction house within a few weeks after the auction.

proof: A coin struck by the Mint specifically for collectors to save. Proof coins are struck twice on specially polished dies and specially selected planchets to assure a chromium-like brilliance.

prooflike: A coin made by the Mint for circulation that looks like a proof. A prooflike coin has similar reflective properties to a proof.

Quarter Eagle: A U.S. $2.50 gold coin, issued from 1796 to 1929.

R1, R2, R3, etc.: A scale of coin rarity ranging from R1 (very common) to R8 (unique).

raw: A coin that has not been certified by a grading service.

RB: Abbreviation for Red Brown designation for copper coins that exhibit coloring between brown and red.

RD: Abbreviation for the red coloring designation of copper coins. Where the slang "red cent" is derived from.

Red Book: Nickname for the annually published *A Guide Book of United States Coins*, by Richard S. Yeoman, the longest-running and, arguably, the most authoritative coin-pricing guide.

reeded edge: A term used when the side of a coin has raised ridges. These were placed on gold and silver coins to discourage removal of metal and continue to be used on some coins that contain no precious metal.

regional show: A coin convention attended by dealers from a number of nearby states.

registry set: A set of coins assembled for inclusion in the Set Registry program of the Professional Coin Grading Service (PCGS) or a similar program of another grading service.

relief: The portion of a coin's design that is raised above the smooth surface, or field.

restrike: A coin made years after the original edition but from the same dies.

reverse: The back or "tails" side of a coin.

rim: The raised ring that borders the obverse and reverse sides of a coin and protects it from wear.

rip: A coin bought for considerably below its real value.

roll: A stack of coins of the same denomination, year, and mint mark. The number of coins composing a roll is often (but not always) fifty.

Saint-Gaudens: Augustus Saint-Gaudens (1848–1907), the designer and engraver for the U.S. Mint of the famed twenty dollar gold eagles, known as the twenty dollar St. Gaudens.

series: A collection that includes one example of each coin date and mint mark issued for a specific type of coin design.

sharp strike: A coin that exhibits strong surface detail because of heavy force at the time the coin was made.

Sheldon: The late Dr. William Sheldon, author of *Penny Whimsy*, the book about large cents in which the coin-grading scale of 1 to 70 was introduced.

slab: A plastic, tamper-resistant holder in which a coin is sealed.

slabbed: A coin that has been graded by a grading service and encapsulated in a plastic holder.

slider: A lightly circulated coin that appears to be uncirculated.

SMS: An acronym for Special Mint Set, a coin set sold by the U.S. Mint from 1965 to 1967.

specie: Coined money, as opposed to paper money or other store of wealth.

spot price: The real time, negotiable price of a commodity.

starred edge: The edge of a coin featuring either raised or sunken stars.

State Quarter: One of a series of special quarter dollars issued by the U.S. Mint in its 50 State Quarters Program. The reverse of each coin bears a commemorative design honoring one of the fifty states of the Union.

stick: A term used by mail-order coin dealers, usually referring to an overpriced and less-than-desirable coin sold through the mail and not returned for a refund by the buyer.

striations: Light patches of a raised scratchlike texture on a coin that result from polishing of a die.

strike: The action of producing a coin, or the quality of a coin's detail sharpness.

switch: Occurs when a less expensive coin is substituted for a valuable coin by an unscrupulous person.

table: A booth at a coin convention rented by a dealer from which to conduct business.

TOCOM: The Tokyo Commodity Exchange.

toning: A slow, natural, regular process by which a coin oxidizes over a period of months and years.

trade dollar: A special type of silver dollar made from 1873 to 1885, primarily for export.

Trime: A U.S. silver three-cent piece, issued from 1851 to 1873.

type: An example of a major design of coin (e.g., Barber quarters and Liberty Seated halves).

UC: Abbreviation for Ultra Cameo designation of a coin that has unusual luster.

uncirculated: A coin that has never circulated or been spent and, most importantly, has no wear.

underbidder: The person bidding on an auction lot in an unreserved public auction who does not bid high enough to acquire the coin he or she is seeking, but whose bids are second-highest.

undercounting: An unscrupulous practice by which, for example, forty-nine coins are sold as a fifty-coin roll.

undergrading: Placing a coin in a lower grade than it actually deserves.

vest-pocket dealer: A dealer who goes to coin shows with an inventory of coins in his or her vest pocket. Vest-pocket dealers rarely take tables at coin shows and often deal in coins on a part-time basis.

view: A pre-sale examination of coins to be sold at auction at a later date. During this viewing, prospective buyers have the opportunity to assess a coin's suitability, grade, authenticity, etc.

virtually: A popular term used to gloss over a coin's shortcomings. "Virtually free of scratches" means the coin has scratches.

weak strike: A coin produced without sharp detail; a weakly struck coin may appear worn, but is still considered Mint State if the lack of detail is from the way it was made, not from subsequent use.

wear: The smoothing or abrading of a coin's top layer of metal caused by circulation.

whiz: To artificially simulate mint luster by removing the top layer of a coin's metal with a circular wire brush and/or abrasive chemical that ultimately alters the coin.

wire rim: A fine, raised line of metal around the rim of very sharply struck coins.

INDEX

Albanese, John, 44, 45–54
American Buffalo gold bullion coins, 118
American Eagle gold bullion coins, 117, 118
American Numismatic Association (ANA), 42
American Numismatic Association Certification Service (ANACS), 101
American Numismatic Society (ANS), 72
Art market, 40
Asset class status of coins, 47–48

Bank of England, 34
Barber dimes, 145
Barber half-dollars, 149
Barber quarter-dollars, 147
Base metal alloy coins
   composition of specific coins, 80
   errors in, 85–86
   as fiat currency, 80
   forecasts for base metals, 87–88
   manganese in, 82
   melting of coins, 83
   nickel in, 81, 87–88
   production of, 84
   State Quarters Program, 84–85, 86
   volatility in base metals, implications of, 82–83
   zinc in, 81, 82, 87

Berkshire Hathaway holding company, 93–94
Bernanke, Ben, 5
   anti-deflation strategy, 20–24
Bimetallic monetary standard, 90
Bonds, ten-year performance record of, 39
Brenner, Victor D., 75
Bre-X Minerals mining company, 115–116
Broadstrike errors, 85
Brown, Gordon, 34
Bryan, William Jennings, 91, 92
Buffalo Head nickels, 144
Buffett, Warren, 93–94
Busang deposit, 115–116

Capped Bust dimes, 145
Capped Bust Eagles, 157
Capped Bust Facing Left Quarter Eagles, 153
Capped Bust Facing Right Quarter Eagles, 153
Capped Bust half-dollars, 148
Capped Bust half-dollars (reeded edge), 149
Capped Bust Half Eagles, 155
Capped Bust quarter-dollars, 147
Capped Draped Bust Facing Left Half Eagles, 155
Capped Head Half Eagles, 156
Capped Head Quarter Eagles, 153
Cash4Gold company, 126

Central banks, 8
Cents
  coin specifications, 141–143
  history and value of, 72–76
Certified Acceptance Corporation (CAC), 44, 45–54
Certified Bullion, 62
Chiu, Cosmos, 105
Classic Head Half Eagles, 156
Classic Head Quarter Eagles, 154
Clayton, Bret, 77
Coinage Act of 1792, 90, 159–169
Coinage Act of 1873, 90
Coinage Act of 1965, 82
Coin collecting, 5–6
Coin-flation, 82
Coin grading
About Good (AG) grades, 44
  About Uncirculated (AU) grades, 43
  art and science of, 55–56
  asset class status of coins and, 47–48
  CAC and its role, 45–54
  coin-grading services, 44, 55
  counterfeit holders and, 59
  Extremely Fine (EF) grades, 43
  Fine (F) grades, 43
  Good (G) grades, 44
  grade-flation problem, 44–45, 48–50
  grading system overview, 42
  holdering of coins and, 56–57, 59
  Mint State (MS) grades, 42–43
  NGC and its role, 57–59
  qualifications used to designate a coin, 42
  stickering of coins, 45, 48, 50
  Very Fine (VF) grades, 43
  Very Good (VG) grades, 44
Coin specifications

cents, 141–143
  dimes, 145–146
  dollars, 150–153
  Double Eagles, 158
  Eagles, 157
  half dimes, 143
  half-dollars, 148–150
  Half Eagles, 155–156
  nickels, 144
  quarter-dollars, 146–148
  Quarter Eagles, 153–154
  silver dollars, 150–152
  "Stellas" (four dollar gold pieces), 155
  three-cent pieces, 143
  three dollar gold pieces, 154
  twenty-cent pieces, 146
  two-cent pieces, 143
Collectors Universe, 73
Commodities, ten-year price performance of, 37–38
Confiscation of gold by the government, 122–124, 169–173
Cooper, Barry, 105
Copper
  bullion purchases, 77
  coins, history and value of, 72–76
  demand for, 71–72
  Exchange-Traded Funds, 76–77
  forecast for, 77
  history of, 70–71
  hybrid car engines and, 70
  ten-year price performance, 71
  thefts of, 70
Copper Development Association, 70
Corn prices, 37
Coronet Eagles, 157
Coronet Half Eagles, 156
Coronet Quarter Eagles, 154

"Cracking out" arbitrage practice, 119–121
Credit rating of United States, 18–20
Cupronickel, 80
Currencies, life and death of, 15–16

DALBAR Inc., 31–32
Debt situation of United States, 18–20
Deficit spending, 10, 16–18
Deflation, 20–24
Dimes, 145–146
Dollar, status and future of, 14–16
Dollar coins, 150–153
Dollar Index, 14–15
Double Eagles ($20.00 pieces), 158
Double-struck coins, 85
Dow Jones Industrials, 4, 30
Draped Bust dimes, 145
Draped Bust half-dollars, 148
Draped Bust Heraldic Eagles, 112
Draped Bust quarter-dollars, 146
Draped Bust silver dollars, 97, 99, 150
Dugan, Gary, 6, 131

Eagles ($10.00 pieces), 157
Eisenhower dollars, 100, 152
Errors in coins, 75–76, 85–86
Exchange-Traded Funds (ETFs)
    copper, 76–77
    gold, 119
    platinum, 138
    silver, 102–104

Federal Reserve System, 7–9, 18
Fiat currency, 9, 10–14, 80

50 State Quarters Program, 84–85, 86
Flowing Hair half-dollars, 148
Flowing Hair silver dollars, 150
Flying Eagle cents, 74, 142
Flynn, Phil, 128
Four dollar gold pieces, 155
Franklin half-dollars, 98, 150
Freeport-McMoRan Copper & Gold, 114, 115

Ganz, David, 123–124
Gobrecht silver dollars, 151
Gold
    betting against United States and, 52–53
    bimetallic monetary standard, 90
    Bre-X scandal, 115–116
    central bank gold sales, 33, 34
    confiscation by the government, 122–124, 169–173
    "cracking out" arbitrage practice, 119–121
    demand for, 6–7, 109–111
    different prices in different forms, 113
    dollar-gold relationship, 108
    forecasts for, 127–131
    gold-versus-silver controversy in U.S. monetary system, 90–93
    as hedge against worst-case scenarios, 108
    history of, 108–109
    investing in, 118–122
    Kingsland Gold and Silver Asset Index, 67
    mining trends, 2, 114–116
    Mint's policy on, 117–118
    new collectors, tips for, 61–62
    Roman gold aureus, 11–12
    selling gold, tips on, 125–126

Gold *(continued)*
  sewer gold, 117
  silver-to-gold ratio, 94
  ten-year price performance, 32–34, 37, 59–60
  TV and phone marketing of, 121, 122
  two-tiered gold market, 112–114
  as under-owned relative to other assets, 61
Gold Bullion Coin Act of 1985, 173–177
Gold dollars, 153
Gold Exchange Traded Fund, 119
Gold standard, 12–13
Grasberg mine, 114
Griffin, G. Edward, 8–9
Guzman, Michael de, 116

Half cents, 141
Half dimes, 143
Half-dollars, 148–150
Half Eagles ($5.00 coins), 155–156
Hill, John H., 129–130
Hishikari Mine, 117
Holdering of coins, 56–57, 59
Home prices, 3
Hunt, Nelson Bunker and Herbert, 93
Hyperinflation, 11

Indian Head cents, 74, 142
Indian Head Eagles, 157
Indian Head Half Eagles, 156
Indian Head Quarter Eagles, 154
Inflation, 9, 10–11, 13–14
  in base metals, 82

International Nickel Study Group (INSG), 87–88
IShares Silver Trust, 102–104

Jefferson nickels, 80, 82, 144
Jobs creation, 4
Johnson Matthey company, 138
J.P. Morgan company, 116
Junk silver, 100–101

Kennedy half-dollars, 80, 100, 150
Kingsland Collectibles Indices, 66–67

Large cents, 141
Legislation, coin-related, 159–177
Lehman Brothers company, 116
Liberty Cap cents, 73, 74
Liberty Head Double Eagles, 158
Liberty Head nickels, 144
Lincoln cents, 74–76, 80, 142
London, Jack, 108–109

Mailing of coins and valuables, 86
Malek, Bert, 127
Manganese, 82
McKinley, William, 91–92, 93
Melting of coins, 83
Mercury dimes, 146
Mint, U.S., 82–83, 84, 117–118, 122
Modern proof sets, 62–63
Mohr, Patricia, 77
Monetary base statistics, 17
Money
  deflation and, 20–24
  dollar, status and future of, 14–16

Federal Reserve and, 7–9
fiat currency, 9, 10–14, 80
inflation and, 9, 10–11, 13–14
Roman money, 9–10, 11–12
Morgan silver dollars, 94, 98–99, 120, 151
Morgan Stanley company, 104–105
Moy, Edmund, 83

Nickel, 81, 87–88
   ten-year price performance, 36
Nickels (five cent pieces), 144
Nixon, Richard M., 12
Numismatic Guaranty Corporation (NGC), 44, 57–59

Obama, Barack, 5
Obama coins, 122
Off-center coins, 85
Oil prices, 38

Panic of 1893, 91
Peace silver dollars, 151
Platinum
bullion coins, 137
   exchange-traded platinum notes, 138
   forecast for, 138–139
   industrial demand for, 134–135
   in jewelry, 135
   mining of, 135–137
   price fluctuations, 136–137
   rarity of, 134
   ten-year price performance, 35–36
Precious metals, intrinsic value of, 28
Presidential dollars, 80, 82, 84, 86, 152

Presidential election of 1896, 91–93
Professional Coin Grading Service (PCGS), 44, 58, 72, 100
Professional Numismatists Guild (PNG), 122

Quantitative Analysis of Investor Behavior (QAIB), 31–32
Quarter-dollars, 146–148
   State Quarters Program, 84–85, 86
Quarter Eagles ($2.50 coins), 153–154
Quast, Brian, 105

Reade, John, 130
Real estate, 2, 3
   outlook for, 38–39
Recession of 2008–09, 2–5
Reserve currency, 14–15
Rio Tinto Group, 77, 114
Rogers, Jimmy, 5
Roman money, 9–10, 11–12
Roosevelt, Franklin, 122
Roosevelt dimes, 80, 82, 146

Sacagawea dollars, 80, 82, 84, 152
Saint-Gaudens Double Eagles, 110, 120, 121, 158
Salzberg, Mark, 54–64
Seated Liberty dimes, 145
Seated Liberty half-dollars, 149
Seated Liberty quarter-dollars, 147
Seated Liberty silver dollars, 151
Service, Robert W., 108–109
Sewer gold, 117
Shield nickels, 144
Shipping of coins and valuables, 86

Silberblatt, Selwyn, 104–105
Silver
  bimetallic monetary standard, 90
  bullion, 96–97
  coins, 97–100
  early history of, 90
  Exchange-Traded Funds, 102–104
  forecast for, 105–106
  gems in pocket change, 101
  gold-versus-silver controversy in U.S. monetary system, 90–93
  investing in, 96–104
  junk silver, 100–101
  Kingsland Gold and Silver Asset Index, 67
  Roman denarius (silver coin), 10, 11, 12
  "silver bug" activities, 93–94
  silver-to-gold ratio, 94
  storage of, 104–105
  supply and demand conditions, 6–7, 95–96
  ten-year price performance, 32, 34–35, 37, 94
  volatility of silver market, 53–54
Silver-center cents, 101
Silver dollars, 150–152
Silver Supply Institute, 95
Sinclair, Jim, 108
Sperber, Laura, 98
Standard & Poor's 500 (S&P), 30–31
Standing Liberty quarter-dollars, 147
State Quarters Program, 84–85, 86
"Stellas" (four dollar gold pieces), 155
Stocks, ten-year performance record of, 29–32
Storage of metals, 104–105

Strawberry Leaf cents, 72
Stuppler, Barry, 128
Susan B. Anthony dollars, 152

Three-cent pieces, 143
Three dollar gold pieces, 154
Trade dollars, 152
Trading with the Enemy Act of 1917, 123
Travers, Scott, 6–7, 25
Turk, James, 106
Twenty-cent pieces, 146
Two-cent pieces, 143

UBS E-TRACS CMCI Long Platinum Total Return fund, 138

Vanguard 500 Fund, 29–30

Walker, David, 9
Walking Liberty half-dollars, 149
Walsh, David, 115
Wark, Graham, 129–130
Washington quarter-dollars, 80, 148
Wheat cents, 75
World Gold Council, 109, 114, 117

Yanachocha mine, 114

Zielinski, Michael, 118
Zimbabwe, 11
Zinc, 81, 82, 87

ACKNOWLEDGMENTS

First, I want to thank my wife, Melissa, and my children, Rachel, Benjamin, and Nathan, for allowing me the time to slip into my office for the many hours that it took to create this book. My mother, Choon Ja (June) was also a constant inspiration to me as was my brother Robert. A special thanks to Scott Travers for not only writing the foreword, but for being the good friend that he is.

At Random House, thanks to Tom Russell for believing in this project and seeing it through, and my greatest thanks to Alison Stoltzfus and for the wonderful editing skills of Shannon Kelly. Mark Salzberg at NGC and David Hall at PCGS gave invaluable access to reference material for which I am grateful. The wonderful legal mind of David L. Ganz, a prolific coin writer and author, also proved invaluable.

I wish to thank New York City Mayor Mike Bloomberg for personally hiring me and giving me the opportunity to report on metals and rare coins for the decade I was employed as a news anchor on his Bloomberg Radio. At the Fox Business Network, I'd like to thank Kevin Magee, Brian Jones, Diane Brandi, and Ray Hennessey for giving me permission to write this book and to attend coins shows. Bob Hoenig and Rich Zaharadnik, my fellow Fox Business Assignment Desk friends and colleagues, deserve a word of thanks for putting up with me and my overloaded schedule during the writing of this book. Thanks also to *Coin World* editor (and former *New York Times* coin columnist) Ed Reiter for his editorial advice. And last but not least, I am especially grateful to John Albanese, coin collector extraordinaire, founder of CAC and NGC, for the time he's taken to give his perspective for this book.